C000010320

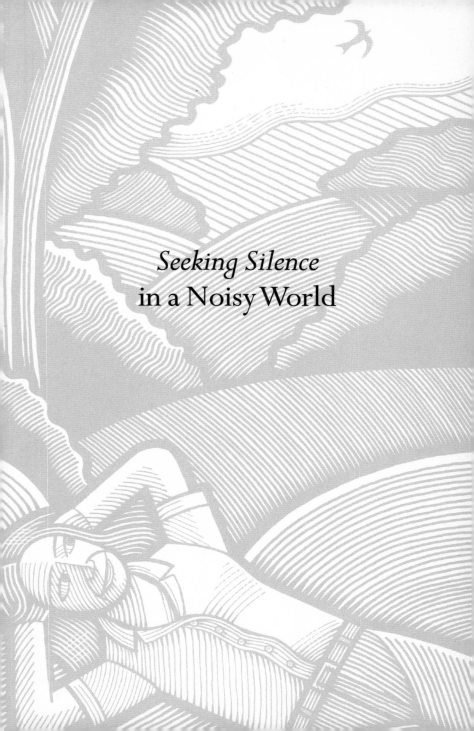

Seeking Silence
in a Noisy World

Seeking Silence
in a Noisy World

The Art of Mindful Solitude

Adam Ford

Leaping Hare Press

First published in the UK in 2011 by

Leaping Hare Press

210 High Street, Lewes
East Sussex BN7 2NS, UK
www.leapingharepress.co.uk

Text copyright © Adam Ford 2011
Design and layout copyright © Ivy Press Limited 2011

All rights reserved. No part of this book may be
reproduced or transmitted in any form or by any
means, electronic or mechanical, including
photocopying, recording or by any information
storage and retrieval system, without written
permission from the copyright holder.

British Library Cataloguing-in-Publication Data
A catalogue record for this book is available from
the British Library

ISBN: 978-1-908005-11-3

This book was conceived, designed and produced by

Leaping Hare Press

Creative Director PETER BRIDGEWATER
Publisher SOPHIE COLLINS
Commissioning Editor MONICA PERDONI
Art Director WAYNE BLADES
Senior Editor JAYNE ANSELL
Designer RICHARD CONSTABLE
Illustrator CLIFFORD HARPER

Printed in China
Colour Origination by Ivy Press Reprographics

10 9 8 7 6 5 4 3 2 1

CONTENTS

INTRODUCTION

*The pleasure of silence has to be one of the
most democratic of experiences — available to
everyone in a noisy world; young or old, rich or poor,
religious or secular. Silence is always there, hovering
quietly in the wings of our lives waiting to be
enjoyed. It can be a solace in times of stress, helping
to regenerate our spirits; it can also be a source
of great creative energy, as artists and writers
have found down through the ages.*

SILENCE, A SPIRITUAL EXERCISE

◆

A generation ago it was unusual to hear of someone going on a retreat. The idea of submitting oneself to an imposed silence in some dry religious cloister seemed, to many people, quite a strange and negative thing to want to do, associated with monks and nuns and a rejection of the world; almost unnatural.

TIMES HAVE CHANGED. Nowadays it has become as normal to go away on a weekend's retreat as it is, perhaps, to spend time on a health farm or enrol in a yoga class. Seeking silence in a busy, noise-filled life has become a spiritual exercise sought out by many people, both religious and secular. Silence has no faith boundaries and can be explored as well by the atheist as by the believer.

Interrogating the Silence

The significance of silence, both as a solace and as a creative power, only dawned on me quite late in life – although it had always been an unacknowledged companion. It happened when listening to an interview on Radio 4 while driving; they were discussing the life of the Orcadian poet George Mackay Brown. I once had the very good fortune to meet the man in Stromness in Orkney – he was a lovely gentle character, who took delight in hearing where a friend and I had been walking on the island of Hoy. In his storytelling and poetry he had an extraordinary talent for describing the low-lying islands of Orkney, their people and the ever-present sea, the wind, the gulls and the seals. The interviewee was talking about George and his writing, and how the poet would seek inspiration while sitting at home in Stromness, as the small fishing town was buffeted by the ocean and North Atlantic gales. He would stoke his peat fire and then sit quietly 'interrogating the silence'.

The Value of Silence

I have carried the phrase 'interrogating the silence' with me ever since, like a quiet mantra. Silence is something so obvious, so available, so 'everyday'. Most of the time we don't recognize its value or even bother to name it; and yet silence is where peace, creativity, self-knowledge, inner strength and even power comes from. When I think of George 'interrogating the silence' it helps me review my own experiences of solitude and loneliness, prayer and meditation in a new light. Silence: the companion at my elbow.

We all share a great ability for ignoring the obvious in life, for not recognizing what is quiet and good. Perhaps the busyness and turmoil of the world, both around us, and also within, the noise and bustle of modern life, the stress, the speeding time, all make it harder for our generation to appreciate the value of silence than it was for our forebears. It would be easy for us to blame the noise and the world for our frustration, but that would get us nowhere.

The Parable of the Cloak

A parable of the Buddha says it nicely. The original story is told in the *Lotus Sutra*, a major text in the Mahayana tradition. A rich man had a son who came of age and planned to set off to explore the world and perhaps find his fortune. The hidden – or not so hidden – anxiety of a parent at this episode in family life is universal. How can I protect my child, how can I shield him or her from the real dangers out there? Tell him to keep in touch, to email regularly? Insist that she contacts a remote cousin she has never met? Slip him an extra $50 note to hide away in his socks for an emergency? In the Buddhist parable the rich man gives his son a cloak.

The cloak is of course both a comfort and a protection against heat and cold; a wonderful, practical and loving gift from a father. What the son doesn't know, however, is that sewn deep into the lining there is hidden a jewel, a gemstone of great value. One day, maybe far in the future when falling on bad times, he will need the jewel, and the father's love will once more reach out and protect him.

Silence, the Hidden Gem

In the *Lotus Sutra*, the hidden gem, carried unknowingly by the boy in his cloak wherever he goes, is Buddhahood, that ultimate Enlightenment which all who follow the Buddhist path in the Mahayana tradition hope for. It is the great awakening to knowledge that is to be found even beyond nirvana.

I think the silence in our lives is rather like this gem —
ever close, a hidden secret, unrecognized most of the time
but always available (with a little thought) and there to be
cherished and enjoyed. It doesn't require a great pilgrimage
(though that can be good) or a heroic spiritual ordeal in a
monastery (which can also be good in its own way, for the
right person) for us to get to know silence. We can find it in
our own neighbourhood, on a walk or at home. We can even
find it beneath the noise.

Why I have Written this Book

My aim in writing this book is not to decry the noise pollution of the modern world (though that can sometimes present
a problem), because there is so much to be gained from living
in these extraordinary times. For many of us, noisy and busy
though our lives may be, silence is still there in the intervals
and in unexplored moments. Having become alert to the true
value of solitude and silence, I will begin by recollecting
some of my own experiences, my failures, unacknowledged
successes, and half-baked attempts at being on retreat (even,
briefly, in a monastery!).

The Quest for Silence

The search for silence is an age-old need and can be found
in all cultures and all periods of history, both ancient and
modern. We have records, extending back over millennia,

of people who made heroic spiritual journeys into solitude, quitting their families, friends and livelihoods just to find silence – in the desert, on mountain tops, in caves, or deep in the forest. Their witness is important to help us understand our own quests, even if their individual experiences go way beyond anything we might dream of for ourselves.

The Darker Side of Silence

We must be alert, too, to the dark side of silence, that too much of it can grind us down, sometimes even be the cause of disorientation and terror. Like the dark, it can spur our imaginations to roam in territories beyond our control. Some people try to avoid silence in their lives at all costs, perhaps subconsciously aware of the possible threat. If only they could find those moments, available to us all, of healing, peaceful silence, they would lose their fear.

There are also far too many witnesses from our own times who have faced a darker side of silence, when it has been imposed upon them by others, suffering at the hands of brutal regimes and the whims of dictators. The torture of solitary confinement and sense deprivation is used as a political weapon; hostages are locked away from the world and used as pawns in power games. Millions live in societies where they are afraid to speak their minds, terrified into silence because those who give voice to their thoughts can disappear in the night.

Finding a Still Point

The main purpose of this book, however, is not to focus on these extreme experiences (though they have their own very important place and will be examined), but to explore simple ways to tease out, to enjoy and to savour moments of silence that are already easily available to us, there in our daily lives. Some will be short, maybe a few minutes identified in a day's routine; others can be as long as a weekend, an impulsive visit to the seaside, or, more formally, an organized retreat. I will also highlight some of the hazards that can be encountered by the beginner seeking silence and suggest ways to avoid them.

We will give thought, too, to the benefits of a simple daily discipline of meditation with some easy instructions on how to get started, making room for a still point in our turning world. My own experience is that the world of Nature is a great giver of good things. Silence is one of them. I think we all need to walk in the woods or over the brow of a hill to reconnect with the world that is our true home.

Enjoy and savour moments of silence that are already easily available to us, there in our daily lives.

CHAPTER ONE

SEEKING SILENCE

*Often we do not recognize the value of silence
until we are driven to seek it; most of the time
it remains an unused resource. My own stumbling
journey, which I will describe throughout the book,
included a formal retreat while I was at college
and a self-imposed silence on a Cumbrian moor.
What I began to discover was that it is the
natural world that helps me most of all.*

Venturing into Silence

◆

Silence is a funny thing; it can be friend or foe. Anyone who has not experienced an extended period of deliberate silence — more than a day, say — should be careful of launching themselves precipitously into silent solitude. It can be hard to handle.

I N THE END SILENCE CAN BE DEEPLY ENJOYABLE, but without preparation and forethought it can be disastrous, or just plain perplexing and lonely. My own early experiences of spending several days in silence can confirm this.

Walking in the woods has been part of my life as far back as I can remember. Woodland holds its own magic silence, enhanced by a bird call, the snapping of a twig, mysterious rustlings, or the stirring of wind in the treetops. For most of my early life I simply took this silence for granted and focused on what I could see, the mushrooms and toadstools, the wood sorrel or the bird I might glimpse. Silence took a back seat.

Silent Night
In my late teens I experienced silence, again incognito, in similar circumstances, when absorbed in the study of something else entirely. I became fascinated with the Moon, built a telescope and spent endless hours of the night out in the cold, absorbed in the mountains and plains, craters and rills of the lunar landscape. I did drawings and compared them with

the observations made by other amateurs. I would return to the telescope with excitement after checking a chart and finding a new feature unmapped before. Sometimes my eyelashes would freeze to the eyepiece as I stood rock still, oblivious to the cold, wrapped in a cloak of silence.

But I did not, I think, give the silence itself a special thought – although I do remember once turning away from the telescope to listen to a woodlark singing in the misty valley below our garden. It was well before dawn. My heart nearly stopped while listening to the silence, waiting for the falling liquid cadences of that lovely bird.

THE 'WHAT AM I DOING HERE?' QUESTION

◆

Many people have moments in their lives when they feel a natural urge to 'get away from it all', to be by themselves in happy silence, where they can sort things out and enjoy some uninterrupted bliss. It does not always work out like that.

A COMMON DOUBT THAT MAY AFFLICT us when we are seeking silence is a feeling of purposelessness. We may have joined a formal retreat or simply be spending a weekend on our own. A cold draught blows through our thoughts and we are assailed by the question, 'What am I doing here?' We have not yet discovered either the solace of silence or the exciting wells of creativity that lie deep within it.

Filling Silence

It was while I was at university that I decided to spend a week on my own, in silence, 'doing some writing'. It seemed a good idea at the time and was fuelled by some romantic and adolescent notions about finding the meaning of life. I borrowed a friend's cottage, one of two empty cottages on a track by an unoccupied farm above Devoke Water on Birker Moor in the western fells of Cumbria. What I discovered was that a long period of silence without a plan can be a problem.

The odd part of this episode, in recollection, was that I had no idea what I was going to write about – there was no burden of thoughts or ideas I was keen to unravel, no novel waiting to see the light of day. True, I had become used to writing down passing ideas or quotes in an exercise book, sometimes a philosophical thought or a haiku; but there was nothing planned for the week ahead.

What Next?

I hitchhiked to Eskdale and then walked up onto the moor, a bleak landscape of rough tufted dead grass and bracken, clumps of reeds by the burbling becks and in the bogs; mounds of moss, clumps of heather, old broken stone walls and exposed shoulders of weathered rock. Sheep roamed freely. The moor is a blissful place on a sunny day, full of colour, rich russets and ochres, wonderful beneath a blue sky; but grey, dismal and desolate in the rain. I arrived in the rain.

There was plenty of silence, if you don't count the bleating of sheep, the croak of ravens and the rattle of the windows. My problem was that I had no tasks to do, nothing to get on with. And that was a recipe for – well, not exactly disaster, but certainly for a nagging and lonely emptiness.

No Purpose in Mind

Unlike Adam Nicolson, who records so tellingly in his book *Sea Room* of his efforts to hold the silence at bay while living alone on tiny islands, the Shiants, in the Outer Hebrides, I had no business to occupy me. I had no fences to mend, no vegetable patch to dig, or house to paint. It is this emptiness and fragility, sometimes exposed in silence, that prompts that sickening question, 'What am I doing here?' Nowadays, I would tell myself firmly not to go down that road.

'Whatever the reality, a kind of silence seems to hang about them. It is not silence, because the sea beats on the shores and the birds scream and flutter about you. But it is a virtual silence, an absence of communication which reduces the islander to a naked condition in front of the universe. He is not padded by the conversation of others.'

ADAM NICOLSON ON BEING ALONE ON THE SHIANT ISLANDS
IN THE OUTER HEBRIDES, FROM 'SEA ROOM'
NORTH POINT PRESS, 2002

The silence was not to blame for this, of course; it was my own naive lack of forethought and preparation, my inability, then, to think about how I might use the silence, or about how the silence might have something to give if only I had approached it better.

Brief Encounter

It wasn't all bad on Birker Moor. I made a number of forays down into the valley, climbed one or two peaks and spent hours sitting on an outcropping crag of granite called Seat How, staring either out to sea or inland to the great mass of Scafell and its flanking range of mountains. I only encountered one person during my week up on the moor; she came bumping and bouncing down the track on a farm tractor, a real land girl who stared down at me for a moment. I recognized her but I hadn't seen her for fifteen years, since she sat next to me in the local primary school. We spoke briefly and then she revved the engine and was gone.

Hearing Things…

Some people apparently hear voices or choirs singing when they are spending long periods of time in silence and solitude. That has never been my experience. The nearest I can come to this is when holding the echo chamber of a shell to my ear to hear the distant surge of the sea at Bootle where, as a small child, I first listened in awe to the sound. Or listening to the old car I owned, which produced a diminutive concert of squeaks and creaks, all of which my brain transmogrified into the calling of a chaffinch in a summer hedgerow.

A Disturbing Dream

I did, however, have a problem with dreams and in particular with a dream that got mixed up with daylight. It was towards the end of the week and became in effect my last night on the moor. I had not yet discovered the role that dreams play in the heightened awareness experienced in solitude; I had not expected to find how powerful a dream can become when you are alone. In a later chapter I will explore this aspect of solitude through the accounts we have of the 'vision quest' by Native Americans, the Sioux of the plains, and the Ojibway of the Great Lakes region. In these ancient cultures the purpose of a young man going off into the wilderness by himself was not to 'do some writing' but to dream a telling dream. The dream would give him a name and a role in life.

My dream was not particularly telling or significant, I think, other than reflecting an unexpected anxiety and sense of meaninglessness about my unplanned time in a remote cottage. I dreamed that I woke in the night to hear the wind in the chimney and in the sycamore trees. Downstairs a telephone began to ring, an ordinary familiar sound in most circumstances. Huddled in the dark, I had only one thought – the cottage had no telephone.

Normally, I am not at all frightened of the dark and haven't been since early childhood – in fact, I love the dark, love its shadows and sky. But that night was different. Something in the cottage wanted me to get up and go downstairs; something was tricking me, and the way I saw it, it had to be malevolent. It was a dream and yet on waking I could not shake off the fear; it invaded daylight. I got dressed, ate a hasty breakfast, packed my rucksack and left.

Back to Normality

I had spent too much time in silence with unstructured time and no plans. I had written nothing worth keeping and needed to get back into ordinary life. The dream stayed with me all day and I remember sitting on the train in Whitehaven on my way to Carlisle, wondering when I was going to wake up and find myself back in the dark on my own with something enticing me to go downstairs. Which was dream and which was reality, I wondered, as they became mixed up together.

My week of silent retreat to 'do some writing' had been a complete failure. Or had it? I had certainly learnt a lesson about approaching silence with caution – and with a plan of action. But I had also learnt something else, and it was not until many years later that this began to dawn on me. This discovery had to do with our need to recognize the importance of finding a personal narrative in our lives. I will explore this need, and how silence can help, in a later chapter.

CHOOSING SILENCE FOR ONESELF

We cannot begin to interrogate the silence in our lives unless it is our own decision to do so. In a rather old-fashioned way, it has to be seen as a calling, a vocation. We must feel drawn to enjoy and explore the silence, making our own inner voluntary choice, approaching it with respect and forethought.

M Y NEXT EXPERIENCE of spending a good chunk of time in silence was in very different circumstances, and this time revealed to me how unhelpful it can be if your silence is arranged by somebody else (that is to say, if you are a bit cussed, like me). My first degree was in theology and philosophy and I went on to a year's training for the Anglican priesthood. This involved living in an all-male theological college for a semi-monastic year, with plenty of time for reading and walking. It was part of the college rule to practise total silence after the evening service, Compline, until the end of morning prayers – 9.30pm until 8.30am not talking, every day for a whole year. At the age of 23, I found myself indulging that familiar question, '*What* am I doing here?'

I hadn't chosen the rule of silence voluntarily – it just came with the package and I think I resented it. It turned out, in fact, to be quite an easy thing with gentle opportunities to read, but it was supposed to have spiritual value and I'm afraid that, at the time, that side of it just passed me by.

Lenten Retreat

It got worse when we reached the season of Lent. A week's retreat for the whole college community loomed ahead and I had to have a strategy to cope. I planned to take a regular daily walk; often I would wander as far as a low hill on the horizon with an Iron Age fortification around the top. Cley Hill was a feature of the local landscape. I also decided to read in translation the whole of Dante's *Divine Comedy: Hell, Purgatory and Paradise*. These things gave me tasks to accomplish during the silence, and the daily routine of college gave a regularity of meals, prayer, spiritual direction and readings in chapel, and sleep. And so the week passed untroubled.

I am not the best person to speak about the value of this religious retreat; the imposed silence I found irksome and somehow unrealistic, something to 'get through'; and the silly games fellow students played at mealtimes to get the salt passed to them without talking, or the suppressed mirth in the corridors, plain irritated me.

I Remember Cley Hill...

And yet somehow, something had happened; an aspect of the week stuck with me, memorably, and gave me something to write about. The retreat was chosen for the days leading up to Easter and I was supposed to be contemplating the traditional events of Holy Week, of Maundy Thursday and Good Friday, Jesus' betrayal, rejection and trial. But that is not what I

recollect with any feeling. Forget the college, the silent per-
ambulating students; forget the hours spent in chapel and the
awkward silent meals. It is Cley Hill that I remember.

Cley Hill is a roughly pyramid-shaped chunk of downland
chalk sitting on the underlying clay substrata of the area. It is
almost 250 metres (800 feet) high and a prominent feature
of the Wiltshire Downs, not so very far from Stonehenge on
Salisbury Plain. It was fortified in the Iron Age, leaving that
tell-tale ditch around the top that marks out so many
defensible sites across the south of England.

I became absorbed in Cley Hill daily, morning, noon and
night. For the first time in my life I began to notice how a
natural feature changes its character and even its size, depend-
ing on the light and the time of day, the cloud cover and the
mist. But however it appeared in all its many forms it was
always there, silent and asking no questions.

The Hill in all its Moods

When I wandered down to the vegetable garden before
breakfast during that week's silent retreat, frost still coated
the Brussels sprouts, tough knobbly greens that had survived
the winter in the hard ground, misshapen now like old trees.
Late snowdrops hinted of the coming spring. Beyond the
garden and the hedge, a line of elm trees carried my eye down
to the horizon beyond woodland and hedgerows to the sure
and familiar form of the hill, wrapped sometimes in an early

morning mist. At other times it was caught in blazing sun-shine, while shadows lurked around the college gardens and surrounding meadows. Then its grassy flanks rose up against the sky as though a field had been unexpectedly tipped on its side into the brilliant lemon sunlight, eye-catching and bold.

With the onset of rain and heavy clouds, Cley Hill would turn grey with the charcoal colours of a drawing and at times a hint of purple. Then, with a clearing sky in the evening, it could settle down quietly into the landscape and almost disappear, becoming no more than a low blue hillock on the horizon, dwarfed by local trees and hedges.

Asking No Questions

Venus and Jupiter dominated the night skies on those evenings, shining brightly through branches of the elms even before the apricot glow of sunset had faded from the west, and the dark blue of night spread out from above. A full moon rising in the east cast stillness over the land, and there, still there, was Cley Hill, now softly lit, rising above the low-lying moon-shadows of the surrounding countryside. It was always there; and as I wrote in my untidy journal at the time, 'asking no questions': just there.

I think it was the 'thereness' of Cley Hill that arrested me. It absorbed me in the way the surface of the Moon had absorbed me when I was getting to know its mountains and craters. For all my uneasiness about an enforced religious retreat in a theological college, I had discovered something: silence had enabled me to see and recognize an aspect of the natural world I might have missed: its stillness, solidity and 'otherness'. And this awakening was not so far, perhaps, from the religious intentions of the college.

THE HERD

◆

Sometimes we have to call time on all the noise in our lives. The incessant bustle of family life, the hum of stressful activity at the office, the noise of the city — there are days when it comes to seem relentless and we need to call a stop, to find stillness. A thing as simple as a candle flame can help.

TWO YEARS LATER, I found myself living the life of a curate in the lovely honey-coloured Cotswold town of Cirencester. It was the mid-1960s, when times were changing – music festivals, flower power, free love and the pill. The future glowed with promise and 'leisure time' was about to take over our lives – or so we thought. These mood swings in the culture had an inevitable effect on the lives of clergy and a certain amount of what was then called 'role confusion' entered our lives. What were we for? What moral standards should we hold to? How were we any different from social workers? Did it matter if we really believed in God or not? And who was God anyway?

I worked as part of a small rural team ministry. We kept the discipline of saying the early morning and evening offices in the chapel of the medieval church in the market square, conducted Sunday services, visited the sick, baptized, married, and buried parishioners – then we were left to our own devices. I got involved in raising awareness and money for the Christian charity Christian Aid through sponsored walks, and this in turn led me into getting to know the youth culture of the town. We had the usual youth club, with noisy sixties' bands who made the church hall doors pulsate with sound and our ears ring for days. The noise levels and boisterous turmoil reached a peak when slowly, without intention, the youth club took up residence in my house, like a garrulous flock of starlings changing the site of their daily roost.

The Herd Moves In

I was not averse to this interesting development and indeed it was probably me who encouraged it. I had moved from a basement flat shared with a shy police detective to live in some church property, a four-storey building on the main street. It was a little bit run down and in great need of decorating. The youth group moved in with gusto, gallon cans of white paint appearing on every floor. But that was just the beginning. A tall lad from the cycle shop had an incredible ability for copying drawings by Picasso onto the walls with black felt pens. In the back kitchen he covered every surface with medieval devils from Dutch painter Hieronymus Bosch. Meanwhile, others painted the sitting room ceiling blood red. Over the next few weeks, kids took turns to stand on a chair balanced on a table to cover the ceiling in yellow daisies. More daisies appeared on an old piano painted green. It became an extra seat when thirty would settle on a Thursday evening to watch *Top of the Pops*. The stair well was dominated by metre-high paintings of the twelve signs of the Zodiac.

Noise filled my days for the next three years. The sound of pop music became a permanent background to my life; ironically, one of the favourite tapes played included 'The Sound of Silence' by Simon and Garfunkel!

Simple Rules

No one had to be a member to use the house at 53 Dyer Street. 'Just turn up' was the rule. We called ourselves The Herd. I decided to have no private possessions; kept one room locked at the top of the house for my bed, a chair and a lamp, and kicked everybody out at 10.30pm. The rules were simple, like, 'Wash your own coffee cup'; and I regularly met people in my kitchen I had never seen before – 'Who are you?' they'd ask, when I wandered in from the street. One day a week I closed the house and spent a night and a day with friends who lived outside the parish in neighbouring villages. Thank God for those many good friends! They seemed intuitively to respect my need for some silence.

Mods & Rockers Take Afternoon Tea

Crowd control became an issue. Many of the visitors to my house rode scooters and flew about town in the evening in their fur-trimmed parkas, with flags flying from their vehicles, girlfriends perched on their pillions. They were the 'Mods' and proud of it. In itself this caused no problems. The difficulty was that in the evenings a large gang of 'Rockers', clad in black leather with shining motorbikes, would congregate at the centre of town. The Mods would sit on my doorstep or lean out of the windows and jeer as Rockers rode past. I could see that all this was building for an ugly situation.

I then did a rather risky and curate-like thing. But it worked. I went up to the centre of town and chatted to the Rockers and invited them all for tea the next Saturday afternoon. And I insisted that if the Mods wanted to go on using my house they would have to serve the tea and make the sandwiches. It was a strange event, somewhat subdued and actually quite friendly. The row of motorbikes parked in the street was a sight to be seen; thunderous when they left. From then on, relations between the two groups simmered equitably on a back burner – much to my relief.

Enough is Enough

Noise levels, however, remained a problem and I ached for some silence. My home continued to be a venue for hordes of happily garrulous young people. They crowded the kitchen at all hours of the day, sat everywhere, clambered over one another, joked, shouted and screamed with laughter. They stencilled their names – over a hundred of them – on my kitchen walls. An ebb and flow synchronized with popular TV programmes. They cooked baked beans, made coffee or tea, and (always charmingly grateful) appeared now and then with a trolley-load of necessities from the local supermarket, with which to restock my shelves.

But, as we all know, too much noise becomes intolerable: it is wearing. Feeling drained and exhausted, I began to wonder if I could continue to cope with the way I was living, sharing my home with such a noisy crowd of people. While searching around for ideas, I came up with thoughts of meditation – for me at first (something that would take me beyond the morning and evening prayers in church), and for them. Would they, The Herd, like to try some silent meditation?

A Peaceful Outcome

I was astonished at the uptake, when I first launched the idea. Two dozen of The Herd immediately said 'yes' to the proposal, with surprising enthusiasm. Perhaps it was the timing – it was the sixties; yoga and transcendental meditation were coming into vogue; flower power and alternative lifestyles were causing a stir. Whatever the reason for this noisy crowd agreeing so readily to be silent, it revealed to me that there is an unacknowledged desire for silence in most lives.

Candlelight Meditation

We needed a focus for a first meditation and democratically chose a candle flame. I had explained that the simple purpose of this meditation was to 'taste' the silence. For this it was necessary to have something to look at that would hold our attention so that inner thoughts and distractions could quieten down – then the silence would be easier to hear.

After locking the front door and turning off the downstairs lights, we assembled in a rough circle in the main room on the first floor. Some who knew about it sat cross-legged; most used cushions and leant against the wall. I talked to them a bit about breathing, about posture, and about how to handle vexing or distracting thoughts. I also suggested to them exercises in visualizing a scene or picture if they found their thoughts wandering. A candle burnt on a low central table.

Silence Fell...

Silence settled. The scene was extraordinary; quiet relaxed faces stared at the candle as one might into the embers of a log fire, faces more familiar to me as the restless features of boisterous noisy teenagers. We allowed our minds to relax, letting go of all thoughts as our focus became absorbed in something outside ourselves, the flickering flame of the candle, the central light casting shadows on the walls.

Outside a dog barked in the distance, an ambulance headed out of town to the hospital; voices passed by in the street and a car pulled up at the traffic lights. Inside the room, the lightly flickering flame gently held our attention and the circle of faces remained unmoved for an hour by those external sounds.

'Wasn't it strange...,' commented one girl after the meditation, '...how all those noises outside made the silence seem even better?' We all agreed.

⌇ Imagination in Meditation ⌇

Many people find it hard at first to settle the distractions of their minds while meditating, which is why it can be helpful to focus on a candle flame or a religious icon or the circular pattern of a Buddhist mandala. Another method is to harness the imagination itself. A passage from scripture is often used for this purpose. A good example is the story of Jesus asleep in a boat on the Sea of Galilee (see Mark 4.35). A storm blows up and terrifies the disciples who are with him (even though they are fishermen). They wake Jesus, who stands up and rebukes the storm. 'Peace! Be still!' he commands, and the storm dies down. The meditation method is to visualize this scene in all its detail, working through from the terror of the disciples and the turmoil of the storm to the final words of Christ. After using this method several times, it may be enough simply to repeat the words 'Peace – Be still'.

Meeting the Quakers

We shared this experience several times. Apart from its own value, varying from person to person, there were a couple of spin-offs from those moments of silence with a candle flame, which I had not anticipated; unintended consequences.

This taste of silence led some of The Herd, who sang in the church choir (most of The Herd were not churchgoers), to show an interest in a local community who worshipped in silence, the Quakers, otherwise known since the seventeenth century as the Society of Friends.

An old Quaker meeting house was just around the corner from the Parish Church and several of the Friends were known to me. I explored the contact and this led to an invitation to take a small group of interested teenagers to experience their gathering on a Sunday. After the parish communion with hymns and anthems, sermon and sacrament, followed by a quick cup of coffee, we trooped round to the Quaker meeting house and sat in serious silence in a very different environment. No clergy, no dressing up, no hymns, no communally recited creed. The building was plain with plain windows, no ornamentation and very Protestant in its simplicity. I found myself being deeply attracted to this silent form of Christian worship. Quakers believe that we each face the silence (and God through the silence) alone, but together. Each one of us contains a spark of the divine and if we live believing this we will find it to be true.

Sponsored Silence

The second unexpected development came from a girl who had taken part in a couple of major sponsored walks we had organized in the Cotswolds in support of Christian Aid. Why don't we do a sponsored silence this year instead of walking down to Cheltenham? We investigated the idea and, once more to my surprise, it was well received.

We have always claimed (not knowing for sure) that this was the first big sponsored silence in aid of charity ever to be organized. I borrowed the gym from the local grammar school, and then The Herd plus a flood of others started to collect sponsors from families and friends. Some local school-teachers made bold promises in sponsorship and paid up well. On the day itself I enjoyed the almost miraculous experience of watching over 700 teenagers in absolute silence for seven hours! They drew, they read, they completed school projects and sometimes they winked and smiled.

This was what the noise of The Herd had led to! Their sponsors paid up, and they raised many thousands of pounds for water-drilling projects in India. And this, in turn, led to an opportunity to explore what silence and solitude meant in Asian religion. I had read a lot about yoga and silent meditation, about the stillness of the Buddha and the spiritual discoveries of the Indian scriptures, the Vedanta, composed in forest hermitages, but I had not had time to investigate these things any further. Now was my chance.

CHAPTER TWO

EXTREME SILENCE

*Throughout recorded history there have been
rare and extraordinary people who have gone to
remarkable lengths to find total silence and solitude
— the search has dominated their lives. In the forests
and mountains of Asia, in the hot dry deserts of Egypt
and in hermitages on cold rocky islands swept by
Atlantic gales, these individuals have gone further to
explore extreme silence than we would ever contemplate
for ourselves. We do not have to emulate such hermits,
any more than we need to become an elite athlete,
swim the English Channel or climb Mount Everest to
keep fit. But we can learn from them.*

WHAT IS SILENCE?

Before we go any further we ought to define silence, which is not as obvious as it seems. This is not an easy task, for although we all may use the word often and with confidence there is little agreement when we try to focus on a precise definition.

FOR A MOTHER, THE LONGED-FOR SILENCE might simply mean the peace that comes with the children tucked up in bed; for a factory worker, the quiet walk home down the street after a day deafened by the din of machinery, is silence cherished. We each have our own experience.

It would be bliss itself for many people to be able, at will, to silence their own minds, the inner turmoil of agitated thoughts. It is not just the noisiness of the modern world that can be wearing – the car alarms and sirens, the incessant sound of music in some high street stores and the uninterrupted hum of traffic, the road drills, aeroplanes, and mobile ring tones. We live in a world of physical noise and many have come to think of it as a new form of pollution. Noise becomes the enemy in our lives, generating anger and wearing us down with frustration. But finding silence means, for many people, resting the mind and letting it go blank and has nothing to do with these external sounds. Some people living in cities find silence, paradoxically, through Buddhist chanting, because of its effect upon the mind.

Silence – Something or Nothing?

We have to ask 'Silence from what?' And perhaps 'Silence for what?' And we will certainly all come up with different answers. For many of us it will simply be a matter of not talking – or being talked to.

Perhaps the most negative understanding of the word silence is enshrined in a radio producer's use of the term 'dead air'. An empty silence in a broadcast lasting more than a few seconds is 'dead air' and something to be avoided at all costs; listeners might turn the radio off or, worse still, switch channels. On these grounds, silence would be defined as a gap, a 'nothing happening', between moments of sound. For many people who have never discovered for themselves the solace of silence or its regenerating creative power, 'nothing' might be the definition they would opt for.

A Personal Experience

One of the reasons I am writing this book arose from a discussion with friends about those human experiences that really cannot be filmed for a reality-TV show or documentary. To be marooned on a desert island, for example, you have to believe that there may be no chance of being saved and that there is no one with you to observe your predicament. To be marooned with a camera crew transforms the experience completely and, although perhaps entertaining, is ultimately ridiculous. An observer will always ruin the quality of solitude.

The same is true for trying to film the life of a hermit, someone who renounces society and seeks the privacy of solitude. The camera, the observer, inevitably changes the experience of being in silence, turning it into something else.

So this is something we can say very clearly about silence: it cannot be practised as a pose or done for effect. It is a personal experience, and even when shared with others it is enjoyed privately for its own sake. It can be written or talked about in retrospect but not observed by a third party while being experienced. The hermit does not say, 'Look at me!' And if he did, he would miss the point of his isolation and would cease to be able to find what he was looking for.

The Sounds of Silence

Henry David Thoreau, retreating from society to a cabin in the woods of New England in the nineteenth century, sought a silence in which he could hear the sound of the wind in the reeds. Others would claim that that is not true silence – for a purist, the sound of bird song and waterfall, wind and rain, are interruptions and distractions. They would reject all sounds in their definition of silence.

I am with Thoreau. I can recollect many instances when natural sounds have contributed to the silence, and in their own way been part of it. Walking once, for example, in the Cotswolds, skirting a field, I heard a sound that perplexed me at first – a gentle swish, somewhere in the distance. I wasn't sure of the direction. I stopped beneath an oak tree, waited and gazed out across the large field of cabbages. Slowly the truth dawned. A belt of rain I hadn't noticed was coming my way, swishing louder and louder, pattering the cabbage leaves. Then the oak tree burst into noisy life for a moment as the rain swept past with a short gust of wind. The sound of the rain did not interrupt the quiet of the countryside – it enhanced, even opened up, the silence.

THE INDIAN EXPERIENCE OF SILENCE

Many of the world's earliest religious writings were inspired by meditation and time spent in silent retreat on a mountain or in the forest, in India. Today, Hindus, Jains and Buddhists all seek guidance from the experience of those men and women who chose solitude – and remarkably, what they found was that the silence is vibrant with contradictions.

I WAS PERSONALLY FORTUNATE to have been linked with the work of Christian Aid in Gloucestershire, for India. The Herd and friends, having raised many thousands of pounds through their sponsored silence, wanted to know if the money would be well spent. It was decided that someone should go and check out the various land development projects being funded. I leapt at the chance, was fortunate enough to be chosen, and was allowed time off to travel.

My main task was to inspect and photograph projects funded by Christian Aid and organized at ground level in cooperation with local Hindus and Muslims. Most of the works involved water projects, the building of enormous earth-banked dams or digging wells the size of football pitches. All the deep red earth was removed in handwoven baskets, carried elegantly on the heads of sari-clad women. The colours were wonderful and the sense of community achievement infectious. Children ran about everywhere with freedom for laughter. I saw this sort of optimistic scene many times as I travelled all over India. But not in the state of Bihar.

An Enervated Silence

There was a lingering famine in Bihar at the time; 30 million people faced starvation. It was easy to see how lack of water for irrigation, or simply to drink, could reduce a whole community to silence. People sat listlessly in the dust by the doors of their homes; children had no energy to play. This silence was not something I had anticipated, and I began to see that silence has a dark side. Seeking a valuable creative silence needs good health, a balanced diet, water and restful sleep. None of these were available to the villagers of Bihar. Mercifully the famine passed, whole communities kept alive by handouts of imported grain donated from abroad. Nowadays, India is a thriving economy with good irrigation schemes and has enjoyed a revolution in its agriculture.

A Serendipitous Meeting

All the time while travelling I was able to indulge a growing interest in Indian religion. The simplicity of marble Mogul mosques vied with the rich animal ornamentation of Hindu temples for my attention. But it was the ideas behind these religions that attracted me most of all; the insights of holy men and women who had experienced silence through yoga – and here I struck lucky.

A chance introduction to an Indian politician brought me to his home in Delhi. He was diplomatically busy; but he managed to give me a bit of time and discovered my interest in the *Upanishads*, some of the oldest and most respected of Indian scriptures. 'Well then,' he said, 'you must meet my old friend Dr Radhakrishnan – he is our greatest scholar and translated the *Upanishads* into English.'

Audience with Dr Radhakrishnan

I had been presented with an incredible opportunity. I could never have organized for myself an audience with this retired scholar–statesman who had once been President of India. My Delhi politician wrote me a note of introduction and I set off by train to Madras. I had questions I wanted to ask about the insights of quiet meditation and how they differed from my own Christian tradition; and I wanted to know if Hinduism was able to adapt to the rise of modern science and in particular to Darwin's theory of evolution.

I found Dr Radhakrishnan living in a modest bungalow in a residential area of the city. Armed guards discreetly patrolled his garden. A servant greeted me and ushered me into a large drawing room. I had not long to wait. The man who appeared, wearing a white dhoti, was more like a dignified professor than a famous politician, first president of the largest democracy on Earth. We sat on comfortable sofas and talked.

⌒ The *Upanishads* ⌒

The *Upanishads* are writings sometimes known as the Vedanta, which arose out of the spiritual experiences of men and women who, almost three thousand years ago, withdrew from society to live in forest retreats. They had had enough of the sort of religion that involved animal sacrifices, the noise of big religious ceremonies and colourful processions that were organized by a superior priesthood. They wanted to understand the nature of the human soul and whether reality was a dream or real. This led to the writing of one of their loveliest prayers, recorded in the *Brihadaranyaka Upanishad* ('aranya' in the title is the Sanskrit word for forest):

> From the unreal lead me to the real,
> From darkness lead me to the light,
> From death lead me to immortality.

The Paradox of Silence

The *Upanishads* illustrate well that retreat into quiet solitude reveals how rich and paradoxical the silence can be and how the opposite of a profound truth may be another apparently contradictory profound truth. How we interpret these truths is a matter of temperament. The *Upanishads* were a living source of inspiration for Radhakrishnan and he wrote in the introduction to his translation of the principal texts:

◆

> We are asked to retire to a field or a forest where the
> world and its noise are out of sight and far away, where
> the sun and the sky, the earth and the water all speak
> the same language, reminding the seeker that he is here
> to develop like the things that grow all around him.

◆

One Reality

I have come across this thought in my reading and travelling, more and more – that we are part of Nature, one element in a richly evolving world. This identity with the living world around us, something we are waking up to in our twenty-first century concern for the environment, is already there in the Vedanta. They believed that behind the face of the world, behind all its teeming variety and rich jungle of life (one thinks of the multi-trunked banyan tree with its mysterious curtains of hanging roots, peopled with parrots and monkeys, curling snakes and beautifully decorated butterflies), there is only one reality – Brahman, the World Self or the World Soul. Even all the gods of the established priesthoods – Agni the god of fire, Indra of rain, and so forth – and all the multitude of village gods in sacred trees and rocks, mountains and streams, are all of them just faces of the One, Brahman (whom we in the West call God).

That is You...

This sense of identity goes even further in some of the *Upani-shads*: even your own soul, your Atman, that too is Brahman. Whatever you contemplate, they discovered, whether God or the world of nature, '*That is you*'. This experience of one-ness is universal and attested in the chronicles of silence from mystics of all religious traditions, and none; and in the journals of many modern-day travellers.

We need this message today to help ground us to a sense of belonging in the world of nature; care for it and we care for ourselves; hurt it and we harm ourselves. And with this thought I began, through discussion with Dr Radhakrishnan, to find an answer to my question about how these teachings chimed with our contemporary view of an evolving world explained by science. The *Upanishads* see life as something that emerges from physical matter; and from life, in turn, emerges the consciousness of mind; and from mind, spirit. 'You see,' he said, 'the theory of evolution has nothing to add to that, in essence'.

A Different Angle

Other texts take a different, seemingly contradictory, line
on our relationship to God. Ultimately, they claim, we are
fulfilled not by identifying with the World Soul, 'becoming
one', losing ourselves like a drop of water in the ocean, but by
worship and adoration. In their view, the final truth discovered in deep silence is an encounter with the divine ground
of the universe, God, who remains wholly 'Other'. Through
worship we retain our personal sense of self. The Indian God
Krishna, for example, figures highly in this devotional tradition; he has the central role in the most popular of Indian
scriptures, the *Bhagavad Gita* ('the Song of the Lord').

The Self is Silent

There are other themes. Radhakrishnan quotes a question and
answer between a teacher and his disciple about the mystery
of Brahman. The disciple asks his teacher to tell him about the
nature of Brahman. 'Teach me, Sir,' he prayed. The teacher was
silent, and when addressed a second and a third time he said:
'I am teaching you but you do not follow. The Self is silent.'

I am reminded, here, of the Buddha who was also sometimes reticent, when questioned about what he had learnt
through silent meditation. It is taught in the Zen tradition that
he once gave a silent sermon by simply holding up a flower.
Only one disciple got the point and smiled; from him this
silent message (and the smile) was passed down, wordlessly,

from generation to generation, for a thousand years until it reached Zen teachers in Japan.

The Buddha's Path

The Buddha, through his interrogation of the silence, came to a radically different view from that of many of his contemporaries as to the nature of ultimate reality. For six years he practised extreme self-denial, following in the footsteps of

---

⟞ A Rich Young Prince… ⟝

The story of the Buddha and his Enlightenment is a classic and very well known (it even made its mark on the Christian calendar through a medieval fictional retelling of the story; 27 November is the saint's day of St Josaphat, his name a verbal corruption of 'Bodhisattva', one of the Buddha's titles). A rich young prince, protected from seeing the suffering of the world by his father the king – given everything, wealth, women and all the luxuries he could want – rebelled against his lot. Scenes of old age, disease and death, encountered on secret trips made incognito from the palace, opened his eyes to the realities of life. And then a wandering holy man, an ascetic, caught his attention and imagination. Inspired, he left home, abandoning his pampered lifestyle, to seek the truth; and the rest, as they say, is history.

---

many holy men of his day. The belief then was that the only way to discover spiritual truth was to subjugate the body and all its appetites, taking a very negative attitude to all physical things. Totally otherworldly. For the Buddha, this became a sort of power-driven anorexia, with the consequence that he became so thin that his spinal column could be seen through the thinning skin of his stomach. Many early Buddhist statues show him at this period of his quest for truth.

He was getting nowhere fast and began to experience the sort of dimming and deadening of the mind that I had witnessed among the poor starving people of Bihar. He rebelled once more, this time against the way of extreme asceticism. From then on he adopted and taught the Middle Way: to eat and sleep and exercise sensibly and then meditate.

Enlightenment

Seeking silence, while sitting beneath the tree that became the famous Tree of Enlightenment, the Buddha reached his goal. He had found a way to understand the world and suffering which, to him, made sense.

His most remarkable 'discovery' in the silence set him apart from those other seekers on forest retreat who produced the *Upanishads*. He was not drawn to lose himself in oneness with God, nor was he drawn to worship God in adoration. His mind continued beyond the gods and beyond Brahman, viewing them as products of man's imagination.

He came to the conclusion that there is no divine creator who is responsible for the universe, only the circle of life and death dominated by suffering and the possibility of a way to rise above it all – the Eightfold Path leading to nirvana.

Sharing the Buddha's View

The Buddha was not alone in his atheist conclusions. In the same era of history another man, generally said to be Mahavira, came to a very similar view while meditating in silence. The Jain religion, founded by Mahavira, believes that there is no God, just a long tradition of holy men who down through the ages have come to the same view that human souls are caught up in the world through ignorance and stuck in lives of discomfort. The aim of meditative yoga is to liberate them.

The witness of extreme silence as practised in early India highlights some interesting contradictions, ones that are still with us today. Either God is behind 'all this' and we achieve our greatest fulfilment through worship, or alternatively we are drawn to identifying with the divine and get caught up in a state of blissful 'Oneness'; or more radically still, there is no God, and we have to find our peace in silent acknowledgement of that fact.

Those of us who seek silence today, privately or on an organized retreat, need to bear in mind these contradictory conclusions, as we try to find our own narrative and our own quiet attempt to make some sense of our lives.

CHRISTIAN HERMITS

It is one of the paradoxes of the Christian tradition that a gospel, so centred in community values and the discovery of God's Kingdom among people, should have then inspired so many individuals to retreat from society to the silent desolation of the Egyptian desert, or to live in remote hermitages on lonely Celtic islands.

ONE ASPECT OF THEIR SILENT QUEST will not attract many followers today, I think – their extreme self-denial and abnegation. Instead of taking pride in their individuality, they wanted to destroy it.

The Christian tradition has always been quite clear about the aim of silent prayer and meditation. '*Be still then, and know that I am God,*' wrote the author of Psalm 46. He believed in God as an ever-present Power, an Eternal Presence, hidden beneath the distractions of the world. And St Ignatius, founder of the Jesuits, wrote in his *Spiritual Exercises*, 'The more our soul finds itself alone and isolated, the more apt it makes itself to approach and to reach its Creator and Lord.'

Into the Desert

This belief that God is always here, waiting to be known, must have been one of the main motives that drove early Christians out into the desert to find silence and solitude and then, through this silence and solitude, God. Many may also have seen themselves as following in the footsteps of Jesus and Moses, who each spent forty days and nights alone in the desert in self-discipline learning to listen, discovering the narrative that was to be their destiny.

But there was another theme. Many of them seemed to take a very negative view of humanity, seeing it as deeply flawed and sinful. The body with all its various appetites, in particular its sexuality, was something to be suppressed and finally conquered. They took no pride in their individuality and set out to destroy it. By retreating into solitude and silence, they faced the enemy and struggled with the strong forces of their own human natures, fighting in a battle against 'the World, the Flesh and the Devil'.

A Spiritual Battle

Some hermits took this battle theme further and became infected with a mythology that divided absolutely everything into good and evil – the spirit being good, while the physical body with all its desires was evil. They were taking part, they believed, in a cosmic drama, the spiritual warfare between good and evil, matter and spirit. They wanted to break their own egocentric spirits, reject all comforts of the body, deny their human appetites, and suppress or crush their sexuality.

These attitudes are not very attractive to twenty-first century ways of thinking. We find it hard to identify with such negative views of human nature or the world we inhabit.

True, it can be hard to be a human being – we all must be aware of that. But when we seek silence and interrogate ourselves today, it is not with the sort of language or mythology used by some of those early hermits. We need guidance and direction, and sometimes a lot of help. We are also capable of behaving in atrociously selfish ways. But we are not, on the whole, self-hating and we work with the basic assumption that we are a good creation; and, if we believe in God, that our human nature, with all its appetites, is part of a God-willed evolving world.

Reluctant Heroes

But it is a tribute to our fascination with self-sufficiency, solitude and silence that many of these hermits became so famous. Even in their own day they were treated as heroes and their struggles were believed to give them wisdom and insight. Ascetic Simeon Stylites retreated from the world in the fifth century to live as a hermit at the top of a pillar in a ruined city in Syria. Vast crowds flocked to see him and to hear him speak. They just wouldn't let him alone.

Silence, it seems, has very real things to say about worldly affairs. It is as though the very act of retreating from everyday life from a time clears the mind and helps put things into perspective. Those who enter the silence very often find themselves turning to look at the world with new eyes. They have advice for those who live busy, noisy lives.

~ **Insights of Solitude** ~

Peter France writes in depth about this paradox of the strange attraction of hermits, in his book *Hermits: The Insights of Solitude*. People have always felt drawn to the solitary hermit for his insights into life – they flocked to them for advice, not on how to be solitary or how to face the silence, but on how to get on in society; how to survive family life, how to deal in business. France pursues this phenomenon down through history, from the days of the first Desert Fathers to the startsy, holy men who lived in the forests of Russia in the nineteenth century. He finds wisdom and humour and even advice on cigar smoking and insomnia.

A Scribe's Life

Not all hermits indulge in titanic spiritual struggles. The simple life of silence and solitude can be hard but pleasurable. Many Celtic monks lived quiet lives in hermitages dedicating their time in silence to making copies of the scriptures, producing wonderful works of art such as the Book of Kells, which can be seen in the library of Trinity College Dublin. These hermits clearly did not see the world as an evil place from which to retreat, but delighted in ordinary things. Their manuscripts are richly decorated with little loving drawings of cats and dogs, fish and fowl, peacocks and twisting vines.

SACRED SITES FOR SILENCE & SOLITUDE

◆

We will never know for ourselves, at first hand, what it is like to live at the end of the world or in the desolate reaches of a desert. But by visiting these places mindfully, giving them a bit of time, we can appreciate something of the hermit's experience.

S ome of the islands associated with the Celtic hermits are well worth a visit, such as Iona just off Mull in the western isles of Scotland or Skellig Michael off the south-west coast of Ireland. Sit or wander in silence and one can get a real sense of their lives, taste a little of their solitude, breathe the clean, clear air that they breathed.

Iona

Iona is many people's favourite place (my brother Inigo named his daughter after it) and it hosts thousands of visitors a year. Its attraction has grown since the foundation of the Iona Community through the inspiration of George MacLeod. They have rebuilt the abbey (originally a Benedictine foundation) and made it a focus of pilgrimage in memory of the sixth-century St Columba and for those who wish to visit the graves of ancient Scottish kings (including Macbeth). The Book of Kells is believed to have been transcribed here and taken to the monastery at Kells in Ireland when the monks were threatened with Viking raids. The abbey has become a spiritual powerhouse, a vibrant centre for interfaith dialogue, for meeting people from all walks of life, for joining in with the chores, and for debating the problems that face the world. Communal meals and communal worship help hold the community together. People who visit love to return.

Visiting Iona

Iona is very easy to reach. When I visited the island, I took my car on the ferry so that I could motor slowly through the magnificent scenery of Mull, its heather and its glens. If you want to taste the silence, shaped by the sounds of the winds and the waves, then it would be wise to book quite a long way ahead to stay overnight at the hotel or in one of the island's B&Bs. The tourists flock to the ferry in the evening and leave the island in peace. Then you can walk on your own up the hill or to one of the beautiful bays on whose beaches green marble pebbles can sometimes be found, called Columba's Tears. Everything is close – the island is only five kilometres long. The weather comes in from the Atlantic, bathing the rocks and small fields in sunshine one minute and pounding them with rain moments later.

It can be a delightful mindful exercise to identify with the monks who lived here, in relative isolation, and those who worked silently on illuminating manuscripts such as the Book of Kells. You can visit the site of St Columba's cell (though some see it as simply a shepherd's stone shelter).

Skellig Michael

For those who want a more extreme and wild sense of remoteness and silence, Skellig Michael is the place to go. The island is little more than a pinnacle of rock out in the Atlantic beyond the furthest, most south-westerly tip of Ireland. It can be hard to reach – boat trips from Kerry dependent on the weather, even in summer. But it can be done.

Climb up the steep track from the sea and you will find a short row of beehive huts called clocháns, built stone upon stone. These are the cells where a thousand years ago the monks committed themselves to lives of silence. Each monk lived alone, though they met for prayer seven times a day in the small church that you can also see.

Silence of a Different Order

The changing face of the sea dominates this world; sometimes, rarely, it is calm when its colour shifts from dark and foreboding tints of grey to a milky aquamarine, slowly heaving with an Atlantic swell. On most days, though, the sea pounds the island with an incessant roar, sending up great plumes of white water that get caught by the wind. Seagulls scream overhead, tossed on a gale, and the wind howls and moans through holes between the stones of the cells. When clouds sit on the ocean they can make the mainland invisible; and the powerful currents and undertow of a furious sea make a boat journey impossible. The sense of isolation is palpable.

This is silence of a different order, isolated from society and shaped by the sounds of nature.

I wonder what the monks had to look forward to, what dream sustained them? Strain the eyes on a clear day, and some people have claimed to see, on the far western horizon, at the edge of the sky, the mythical Land of the Young, *Tír na nÓg*. Perhaps the monks dreamed of this paradise that had inspired the Celts from time immemorial, a place of eternal youth, without anxieties, or suffering. Or is it possible they lived and prayed in the present moment without dreams, content and awake in the Now?

Silence in the Desert

The quality of silence in the desert is quite different from that on a remote Celtic island. To share a hint of the experience of the early Desert Fathers, we need to head south. There are travel organizations such as 'Wind Sand & Stars' that specialize in arranging individual desert retreats for those who want a taste of extreme silence. Sara Maitland went with them and describes her experience in *A Book of Silence*. She writes of the barren landscape and the broken rocks; watching the sun arcing across the sky, shifting the shadows; and waking up to find the tiny footprints of scorpions in the sand near her sleeping bag. She sat each day for a week perched on an escarpment by a wadi (a narrow dry river bed) and was overwhelmed by the silence.

Music of the Spheres?

With the absence of anything to hear, in the hot stillness of the desert, we begin to notice a continuous swish, difficult to describe – the rushing and singing sound of our own blood coursing through our veins. I sometimes wonder if it was this mysterious sound that encouraged Pythagoras, the early Greek mathematician and mystic, to invent his theory of the music of the spheres.

Pythagoras believed in the mathematical beauty and harmony of all creation – an early discovery of a principle that guides mathematicians and physicists even today, in the twenty-first century. In the Pythagorean universe, the Sun, Moon and planets all revolve about the Earth in concentric glass-like spheres – in their swift revolution they hum each at a different pitch, producing a glorious heavenly music. Strain to listen hard in total silence and one might catch a hint of those celestial harmonies; but, according to tradition, Pythagoras alone had the gift to hear the music of the spheres.

The wilderness has had a powerful influence on our western ideas of God. Islam, Christianity and Judaism were all born in the desert. Mohammed, Jesus and Moses all retreated into its hot solitary wasteland at some point in their lives and came back from it inspired.

Perhaps in order to understand the language and imagery of these religious traditions, and to appreciate their spiritual core, we should all taste the desert silence once before we die.

ARTISTS IN SILENT PLACES

Every continent has places where silence reigns, and they are worth seeking out. Some are famous, like the Grand Canyon in the USA or Uluru in the Red Centre of Australia; others are less well known and, because they do not attract so many tourists, easily become personal favourites. They invite a pilgrimage.

TWO OF MY OWN FAVOURITE LONELY PLACES have been associated with artists, one in New Mexico and the other in Western Australia. The grandeur of the natural world has often been a potent source of inspiration for sculptors and painters. The American painter Georgia O'Keeffe found pattern and colour in geological formations, while British sculptor Antony Gormley experimented with installations, placing the human figure in unusual landscapes.

The White Place

The first we found almost by accident. My partner, Ros, and I were driving through New Mexico and stopped to visit the house and studio of one of our favourite American artists, Georgia O'Keeffe, at Abiquiú. We loved her mysterious paintings of the Black Hills and her vivid use of colour when portraying the geology of New Mexico – orange landscapes, with purple, mauve and rust-red cliffs. But it was a chance conversation with a couple at the next table in a restaurant that led us to the White Place, one of Georgia O'Keeffe's favourite spots. O'Keeffe captured the atmosphere of the White Place in many paintings, almost abstract in their design.

To get to the Plaza Colorado, which the artist renamed The White Place, *Plaza Blanca*, we drove along a back road from Abiquiú, parked, and then walked into the labyrinthine landscape of the canyon. It was silent and we strolled alone past palisade cliffs and cathedral-like canyons of gleaming white stone, carved into elegant shapes by wind and rain over aeons of time. Weather-rounded boulders perched on gothic pinnacles and pillars of rock. Stunted pine trees grew on the floor of the dried-up riverbed, blue gentian-like flowers clung close to the stony ground. The canyon contained a silence that made one want to whisper.

Antony Gormley in Australia

The second very special place associated with an artist was far more remote and entailed some serious planning before we were able to visit it. We were staying in Perth in Western Australia and wanted to see what we had heard was a remarkable art installation by Antony Gormley.

We took the train from Perth to Kalgoorlie, a seven-hour journey, and stayed the night in a hotel. The next day we rented a land cruiser and drove north over fifty kilometres on dirt tracks past the small mining town of Menzies and on into the outback and to Lake Ballard. Lake Ballard is a lake in the

Australian sense – there may be water in a flash flood once in a decade or less, but most of the time it is a dry salt pan. If you are a European, the remoteness of this parched landscape can be unnerving. Visitors are warned that there are limited facilities available in the area. Take this warning seriously.

Reaching the Site

The scene that greeted us after parking the vehicle and walking down the track to the salt pan was surreal. The heat beat down from a brazen sky, and the horizon disappeared in a mirage, a low smudge of shimmering bush appearing to sit in a sheet of water. Flies swarmed in clouds about our heads.

Gormley had chosen the site because the underlying bed of the salt pan was a great slab of Archean rock, one of the oldest chunks of the Earth's crust to be found anywhere. The Perth International Arts Festival, with a stroke of inspiration, commissioned the work, even though it requires visitors to make a lengthy pilgrimage to visit the site.

Austere Mystery

Standing on the salt pan were fifty-one human-sized naked figures cast from a special alloy made from elements mined in Western Australia. They are so well spread out that we could not see them all at once, each one erect in splendid isolation a hundred metres or so from its neighbour. Although as tall as people, they are thinner (their width reduced by a third);

this somehow adds to their austere mystery. Each figure is different and they are all based upon the dimensions of fifty-one of the local inhabitants of Menzies, who agreed to have their naked bodies scanned by laser. The figures stand in silent contemplation of the horizon, each in its own shimmering patch of the salt pan, some with their feet lost in a mirage. They appear both alien and human at the same time.

A Note of Caution

The impact of making a silent retreat in a desert affects people in different ways. Not everyone is overcome by the beauty of desolate silent places; some hate the empty wilderness.

Brian Keenan and John McCarthy, hostages held together in prison for four years in Beirut, made a fanciful vow that if they were released they would farm yaks in Patagonia. In *Between Extremes* they give an amusing account of a pilgrimage they make together through the length of Chile, rejoicing in their freedom. Keenan finds himself crushed by the nothingness of the barren landscape of a dry salt lake. He becomes angry that deserts are portrayed in literature as places of healing and solitude; 'Every desert mystic ... was a frigging liar,' he wrote. His favourite poet Neruda disappoints him when he reads his romantic response to the Atacama Desert. But just when you think he has written off all wilderness-poets as fantasists, his loathing is overcome by illumination, as he gazes over the fabulous Valley of the Moon.

CHAPTER THREE

THE DARK SIDE OF SILENCE

There is a dark side to silence, which we come across in many forms. The silence itself may carry a threat we don't entirely understand, and fears loom large. Or it may be used by others as a pernicious form of torture in a prison cell. For millions of people in the world today, it weighs heavily as an uninvited guest in their lives, forbidding them to speak freely or openly about things that matter. Political oppression breeds such a suffocating silence.

FEAR OF THE UNKNOWN

◆

Silence, like the dark, can be frightening. We don't always know how to handle it or what it is we are facing. Fear of the unknown is a natural defence mechanism, a warning to go carefully. In a noisy world, the sudden outbreak of silence can be quite a shock.

WHEN I WAS VERY YOUNG we lived in the hamlet of Seathwaite in Dunnerdale, a remote and very beautiful valley in Cumberland (now Cumbria). One day there was a knock at the vicarage door and I raced to answer it before anyone else. A man stood there, running with sweat, exhausted and appearing troubled. Breathing heavily, he looked down at me. 'Is the vicar at home?' he asked.

Two hours later he left.

The Tale of the Methodist Minister

My Dad was very careful about not passing on confidences or gossiping about things said to him in his study (he preached regularly about the destructive effect of malicious gossip in the parish). But this much we were able to gather from him. The exhausted visitor was a Methodist minister from Manchester; he had been having a tough time in the city and had decided to give himself a break and go on a walking holiday, a sort of private retreat in the Lake District. He was on his own seeking a bit of peace and silence.

He had climbed Harter Fell, a pyramid-shaped and rocky peak straddling the moors between Seathwaite and Eskdale. Sitting at the top, happily eating his picnic beneath a blue sky, listening to the silence, he had been suddenly afflicted with an overpowering sense of evil – or what he interpreted to be evil. It terrified him and he fled, running the whole way down the mountainside, through the forest and on down the valley, past the tumbling falls of the River Duddon, to find the nearest sympathetic listener he could think of, the local vicar.

Scared on a Mountain

We tried to make sense of his experience. My mother's view (she also came from Manchester) was that the silence was such a great contrast with the continuous bustle and noise of the city that it was not surprising he found it disturbing. He just wasn't used to it. It gave him a jolt he couldn't understand. Perhaps it brought inner troubles to the surface, which he was unable, for the moment, to face.

I know that as a child I sympathized with him (as I do now in retrospect, but for different reasons) because I knew what it was like to feel scared on a mountain. Not long before, on my fourth birthday, we had climbed Caw Fell on the southern side of the valley. Toiling my way up, I saw an enormous boulder of the local pink granite and became convinced it was a giant wild pig, asleep. We picnicked at the top to celebrate my climb, and my birthday, and then headed home. I trailed behind, not telling anyone of my private fears, dreading the point on the track where I would have to pass the sleeping monster. I never mentioned the threat of the pig for years. Maybe I knew even then that I was being fanciful and enjoyed entertaining the frisson of fear, even though I knew there was no grotesque pig; it was just a rock. I still remember it vividly.

Tuning in to Evil

My father, who was prone to such things, took a much more romantic view of the visitor's experience, if 'romantic' is the right word. He and the Methodist minister had speculated about Druids and wondered whether the rocks on the top of Harter Fell had been a site of human sacrifice. They certainly form a dramatic theatre. Perhaps the suffering and evil of such ceremonies had left an imprint in the rocks and he, being a sensitive person, had picked up on this imprint – tuned in, as it were, to its wavelength.

Certainly the fells around were full of evidences of early settlement several thousand years ago, of farmers who cleared the land for simple agriculture; but no signs, as far as I am aware, of any Druid practices. So I do not go along with this explanation for two reasons. Firstly, I think that the Druids are probably much maligned. We only know of them from the word of their enemies; malicious gossip of one culture putting down another. Secondly, I do not think that the natural world picks up on the horrible things man does to man. Rocks have no memory of our passing evils, nor the flowers, nor the trees. They are innocent. Even if there *had* been human sacrifice or murder on the top of Harter Fell, I am convinced that the rocks know nothing of it. But then I do not believe in a force of evil as such — just the evil things people are able to do to one another out of selfishness, ignorance, stupidity, and a complete lack of a loving or compassionate imagination.

The Frisson of Fear

I have since wondered if the shock to his system of facing silence on his own on a mountain, after living in Manchester, sparked off thoughts about Jesus' temptations in the wilderness. It is a story with which he would be very familiar, as a Methodist minister. We all of us bring so much baggage to the silence, both personal and cultural; he might have expected subconsciously to encounter 'the evil one' when alone in such a place. Perhaps he too enjoyed the frisson of fear that came with the psychodrama, and he was glad in some strange way to indulge it; the devil and evil forces were already part of his religious world view. And so in these terms he tried to rationalize his frightening experience, which, there is no doubt, was triggered by the silence he encountered on that mountain. He wanted to make some sense of it.

We all of us bring so much baggage to the silence, both personal and cultural.

POWERFUL DISTRACTIONS IN THE SILENCE

◆

Silence allows our free minds to range widely, sometimes bringing dark thoughts and temptations to the surface. They can become severe distractions until they have been faced and then dismissed. But we are not alone when afflicted in this way; most of the great religious leaders in history have suffered from the same problem.

THERE CAN BE MANY DISTRACTIONS when seeking silence in a wild place – the deep roar of a low-flying aircraft suddenly shattering the peace, the persistent drone of a distant motorway. But the worst distractions will come from within. Stories of the Buddha's quest for enlightenment and of Jesus' forty days in the wilderness of Judea attest to this.

The Buddha, meditating beneath the banyan tree, was assaulted by Mara the 'evil one', one of whose aims seems to have been to tempt the Buddha to *succeed* in his meditations and discover the peace of final nirvana – with the proviso that he wouldn't come back to teach the world the doctrine of liberation! In other words, Mara represented the selfish desire to go off alone, rejecting all compassionate feelings he might have to help others locked up in ignorance and suffering.

The Army & Daughters of Mara

Buddhist tales are full of popular demonology, gods, and spirits of nature, a rich forest of fantasy, of mythology and of storytelling, even though the Buddha's teaching would take his followers far beyond all that. Mara is the popular face and personification of inner selfish desires. We know this because Mara has an army with which to attack the Buddha as he tries to get some peaceful silence, the names of his soldiers being Lust, Aversion, Hunger and Thirst, Craving, Sloth and Indolence, Cowardice, Doubt, Hypocrisy, and Stupidity. Mara even hits him with a stomach ache in one tale!

In another source this enemy host becomes the three daughters of Mara – Craving, Anger and Lust. They dance before him lasciviously, attempting to distract his mind while he tries to interrogate the silence in peace. The Buddha conquered these temptations, dismissed the army and daughters of Mara, and moved on in his quest for a deeper silence.

Jesus, it seems, had a similar problem.

Tempted by the Devil

We know virtually nothing about Jesus before he appears in Galilee preaching about the Kingdom of God – unlike the story of the Buddha, whose Enlightenment and teaching are preceded by a whole cycle of tales. At the beginning of his ministry, Jesus is said to have spent forty days and nights in the wilderness, alone and in silence, where he is tempted by the Devil. The Devil offers him power – that he could, if he wished and set his mind to it, become a world ruler. Interestingly, this is one of the temptations that Mara lays before the

Buddha. Both men had it within them to become great leaders in a worldly sense. Both rejected the temptation.

In the colourful gospel story, Satan offers him various fanciful powers – to turn stones into bread, to leap from a high place and be saved by angels, to wield naked power over all the nations of the Earth. Jesus and Satan spar with one another by quoting scripture. Eventually, Satan is summarily dismissed and leaves the stage, rather as Mara was dismissed five hundred years earlier by the Buddha.

A Vision of the Wilderness

When I was teaching at St Paul's Girls' School in London, I once set this as an exercise for a class of fourteen-year-olds. 'Imagine you are given a million pounds to make a film of the life of Jesus – how would you film this scene of Jesus' temptations in the wilderness? No expense spared – just think how you would best portray what really happened.'

The results of this imaginary exercise were as varied as I had anticipated. Some had fun with a colourful pantomime devil – cloak, tail, horns and all, with red as a dominant colour. One or two girls opted for cartoon, a medium that offered them more freedom of expression. The majority, however, decided that the Devil was too problematic to portray on screen and decided simply to use a voice over, varying from oily snake through congenial charm to that deep American gruff that one sometimes hears in adverts on TV.

Winning Scenario

One girl came up with an idea, which after class debate was voted the best, involving no extra actors or voices.

'I would have Jesus sitting on a rock, just quietly staring at the ground, watching an ant perhaps. Then I would have his inner double stand up, separating from him, walk over to another rock, where he would sit down and face himself. The temptations would then be a dialogue between Jesus and his inner self-seeking double.'

I liked it. I had just been to see an exhibition of paintings by Stanley Spencer depicting Jesus alone in the wilderness; in one scene he sits in the desert, a gentle thoughtful human being, affectionately contemplating a scorpion. The distractions he faced in the silence of the desert came from within, because it is difficult being a man at the best of times, let alone when facing a great task.

Overcoming Temptation in Silence

Buddha and Jesus, great men both of them, had to confront and overcome powerful inner forces – distractions and temptations, which only revealed their true nature when faced in silence and solitude. One of the most interesting features of their retreats from the world was that the experience drove them both back into the world. Through interrogating the silence, they had discovered a deeper care and compassion for mankind and a mission to give guidance and illumination.

We might match our own limited experiences of silence against this yardstick. Far from taking us off into a private dream, the fruits of silence can be to see the world and other people through new eyes, to cultivate a deeper compassion for, and understanding of, others. The desire to escape, for private peace, gets turned round and becomes the desire to go back to be among people, to be kind and to give help.

Silence as a Weapon

It is a common experience that taking time out, to stand back from the noise and stress of life, can have very positive results. It gives us a new relaxed perspective on things, helps us to get things in proportion; it can liberate those natural feelings of care and kindness for those around us, which can be so easily suppressed by tiredness and anxiety.

But silence, like many other good things, can be turned into a sword, become a weapon which can be used to inflict harm and hurt. Think of how silence can weigh heavily on a relationship or within a family. Some small argument or incident can lead to a sustained sulky silence; a stroppy teenager can make life really difficult for a well-meaning parent by refusing to speak; a judgemental parent can cause real pain by turning away from a child and refusing to talk to them. We are all tempted to use silence in this way at some time or other; 'That'll show them!', we think, with a touch of self-righteousness and vindictive pleasure.

It is a dangerous weapon. It can wither the confidence of the person against whom it is being wielded. It can equally hurt the person who is controlling the silence – even if (and perhaps because) they feel it is giving them the upper hand.

A Very Long Silence

There is a case in point. When I was five years old we moved over the moor from Dunnerdale to Eskdale, from one vicarage to another. As my father got to know his new parish he would sometimes return from visiting remote farms and tell us about the people who lived there. One day he came back from a particularly distant farm on the parish boundary high up on the moors.

'It was a strange place!' he said. 'There's a farmer and his wife, no children, and one farm labourer who walks up from the valley daily. It's a lonely spot at the end of a long dirt track. There was something wrong and unhappy about the place but I couldn't put my finger on it.'

'What do you think was wrong?' asked my mother.

Tell 'er, tell 'im...

'Well – I found out!' he said. 'I had a chat to the labourer. He walked back down the track with me. Apparently the farmer and his wife had had an argument and weren't talking. So I asked him how did they run the farm like that? "Ah...!" he said, "'E tells me to tell 'er, some'ert; like it's time she cleaned the chickens out; and then she'll say, tell 'im he ain't mended the peg on the door." They have refused to speak to each other since the argument apparently. All messages go through the hired labourer.'

'And how long's that been going on for?' asked my mother.

'Twenty years, it seems!'

> *We are all amateurs when it comes to saying sorry.*

Breaking the Silence

Silence of this sort becomes a trap of our own making. There is only one way to deal with it – to break it; but that can be surprisingly difficult. People stuck in such a trap may need professional help from a counsellor, or at least a good listening friend. Handled quickly ('Don't let the sun set on your wrath,' goes the proverb – the same is true for silence inflicted on another), it won't become a problem. We have to find strategies – simply saying 'I'm sorry'; or 'Can we talk about such-and-such sometime?'; or a joke (if appropriate), or a small gift. We are all amateurs when it comes to saying sorry.

PRISONERS OF CONSCIENCE

◆

There can be no breaking of the silence if it has been imposed upon an individual by an oppressive regime. The only hope is that those with power will let go the torture, and a deeper sense of humanity be cultivated among the oppressed, 'beneath the silence'.

IT IS HORRIFYING HOW MANY PRISONERS OF CONSCIENCE there are in the world in our time, and how many are held in solitary confinement, today, this morning, now – this very moment, while I am writing this or you are reading it.

Anyone held in solitary confinement is mute and many of them have stories that remain forever untold. Some, if they are fortunate, come to the attention of the world through the loyal hardwork of friends or by being championed by organizations such as Amnesty International. For over fifty years Amnesty has been repeating its message that prolonged solitary confinement can have serious effects on the physical and mental health of prisoners. Yet a quick trawl of their web site reveals that institutions and governments still use, or turn a blind eye to, this barbaric practice.

We are all Guilty
It would be quite easy to quote the inhumane and squalid conditions in which solitary prisoners are held in some oppressive regimes; it seems that almost all societies are

guilty, despite the work of the United Nations Human Rights Committee. The Israeli nuclear whistleblower Mordechai Vananu was held in isolation for the first eleven years of his imprisonment for revealing details of the country's nuclear arsenal near the southern town of Dimona in the British newspaper *The Sunday Times*. The reason given by the Israeli authorities for this draconian treatment was so he would be protected from other prisoners.

Not all prisoners held in isolation are innocent people, of course. I read today (June 2011) of two men who have been held in isolation in a jail in Louisiana, USA, for forty years. They are confined to their small cells for twenty-three hours a day. When weather permits they are allowed outside three times a week for an hour of solitary recreation in a small outdoor cage. For four hours a week they are allowed to leave their cells to shower, or walk, alone, along a corridor. In jail for armed robbery they were later charged, very dubiously according to lawyers who have looked at the case, with the murder of a prison guard: hence their solitary confinement. No one deserves such treatment.

The trouble is that we all forget – it is one of the problems that bedevil society; our compassion comes in short bursts. We may write a letter in support of our 'favourite' prisoner of conscience, or even of a guilty man who is being badly treated. But then life moves on and we forget that we are all linked; that we live in one world, our silence shared.

SILENCE AS A SURVIVAL STRATEGY

◆

Whole communities can be held in thrall by silence out of fear — of the secret police, of arbitrary arrest, of disappearing in the night, of torture, of being denounced by a neighbour. When a country is ruled by thugs, who can you trust? Better to keep your mouth shut.

BULLYING REGIMES AND DICTATORS HATE CRITICISM. They protect their power by inhuman means, fearful of losing control, paranoid about opposition. The history of the twentieth century is dominated by totalitarian regimes addicted to power. Biographies of Stalin, Mao, Hitler, Idi Amin and many others all tell the same story of millions terrified into silence by ruthless control. It is a theme well documented in novels — one thinks of George Orwell's *Nineteen Eighty-Four*, or Franz Kafka's *The Trial*. The story is repeated again and again, in the twenty-first century, in parts of Africa, in the Middle East and in the Far East.

Even in the USA, the 'land of the free', older citizens still remember the time in the 1950s when anxiety about communism made it difficult for liberal-minded people to speak their minds for fear of being investigated by the House of Un-American Activities Committee. Everyone became suspect. 'Reds under the bed' became the paranoid fear that silenced opinion. Even the most civilized countries should be alert to the bullying power of governments or of the media.

A Literary Look at Silence

Those of us who have the good fortune to live in open democracies where the rule of law holds strong and freedom of speech is valued find it hard to imagine what it must be like not to be able to say what you think. It must be terrible to think of silence as a survival strategy rather than a solace.

I have to turn to an historical novel to gain some feeling and understanding as to what it must be like to be silent day after day out of fear. *Silence* by the Japanese writer Shusaku Endo deals with the period in Japanese history when Christian missionaries were expelled from the country in the seventeenth century and Christianity itself banned under pain of death or torture. European power was growing in the Far East and Japan began to fear it would lose its identity. Jesuit priests from Portugal continued to travel to the land incognito, however, and Endo bases his novel on one such real historical character.

Holding the Faith

Peasants suspected of continuing their practice of the outlawed religion – or even worse, of harbouring priests – were put on trial and made to trample on an image of Jesus and the Virgin Mary. Only a complete denunciation of their faith would secure their release (and often not even that). The tenacity of these poor people and loyalty to their God was quite remarkable. Secrecy, to preserve their faith, ruled their lives. And when they had to suffer, they suffered in silence, without protest.

But there was an even darker side to their silence, which torments the Jesuit priest throughout the story. It is the silence of God. It seemed that God had folded his arms and would have nothing to do with their plight.

Why Have You Forsaken Me?

Two peasants from the village that had protected and hidden the priest were investigated by the authorities from Nagasaki, who were known for their brutality. When the men did not cooperate, they were tied to stakes on the seashore and left there for the tide to come in and drown them. 'Why have you abandoned us so completely?' prays the priest, and he recollects yet again the cry of Jesus on the cross, 'My God, My God, why have you forsaken me?'

He hears the sound of the waves as they break on the shore all night long; the waves that washed relentlessly the dead bodies of the two peasants. The darkness maintained its stubborn silence. It seemed to the priest as though God was as indifferent to the fate of the men as the cold sea itself.

He succumbs, finally, to the terror and tramples on an image of Christ, and in that moment of betrayal and defeat comes to the thought that God had not abandoned him at all, nor the tortured peasants, but was there with them all the time in their silent suffering.

CHAPTER FOUR

THE NATURAL WORLD

*The natural world — our natural home —
is a great source of silence, if by silence we mean
neither talking to other people nor being talked to.
We may not feel like it, when living in our modern
houses in modern cities, with all the noise of
technology and communication, mobile phones and
televisions, washing machines and cars, but we are a
product of nature and we have a deep kinship with
the hedgerow and forest. We have emerged on Earth
by natural organic processes through evolution.
For our good health, and that of the planet, we
need to think about these things mindfully.*

THE TONIC OF WILDNESS

◆

'We need the tonic of wildness,' wrote the New England writer Henry David Thoreau in his book Walden; or, Life in the Woods. *'We can never have enough of Nature.' It was easier then, in the mid-nineteenth century, to get away from it all — there were far fewer people on the planet than there are now, and more open space.*

THE SMALL TOWN OF CONCORD, where Thoreau lived, was enveloped by nature: 'Our village life would stagnate if it were not for the unexplored forests and meadows which surround it.' Friends and neighbours were perplexed by Thoreau's retreat to the forest, suspecting him of sheer idleness and wondering how he could survive without the company of other human beings, fearing he would be lonely in his semi-hermit existence. But Thoreau was following his own path; a line from his book has been much quoted: 'If a man does not keep pace with his companions, perhaps it is because he hears a different drummer. Let him step to the music which he hears, however measured or far away.'

He was far from being indolent, and actually enjoyed hearing the faint sounds of village life that drifted his way on the evening air; he regularly entertained guests who beat their way to the door of his simple hut in the woods; and he liked to hear freight trains rumbling along in the distance (they made him feel, in his hermitage, like a citizen of the world).

'Time is but the stream I go a-fishing in.'

Thoreau's Sanctuary

Thoreau worked hard, though leaving plenty of time for the silent observation and contemplation of nature. He built his airy unplastered cabin for a few dollars from recycled planks, and tended a large field of beans. But what he really enjoyed was the stillness and the solitude. 'I never found the companion that was so companionable as solitude.' He could spend weeks on his own not talking and not being talked to. He wanted above all to 'be awake', alert to the chickadees and wood thrushes, the changing life of Walden Pond from summer to winter; to share the companionship of pine tree, hemlock and willow. 'I went to the woods because I wished to live deliberately, to front only the essential facts of life...' It was the simple life without the clutter of unnecessary possessions or conversations that attracted him. There was no haste or hassle in his life in the woods, no pressure from clock or timetable. 'Time is but the stream I go a-fishing in.'

'There can be no very black melancholy to him who
lives in the midst of Nature and has his senses still.'

FROM 'WALDEN; OR, LIFE IN THE WOODS' BY HENRY DAVID THOREAU
STERLING INNOVATION, 2009

Simple Patterns

It is the simplicity of the solitary silence of the lone observer that makes Thoreau's writings so telling. I have found many of his observations of the beauty and harmony of nature immensely moving. His timeless reflections on simple things are full of a joyful hopefulness – as though we are living in the early springtime of the world.

He scrutinizes the formation of bubbles in the ice of Walden Pond, as winter draws on, with an absorbed curiosity; he sees simple patterns in nature underlying all of its rich blossoming complexity. The spreading rivulets in thawing clay on the railway embankment inspire him to see the same developing patterns in the formation of ice across a window-pane, the growth of a tree or the structure of veins in a leaf. Writing of these 'sand foliage' patterns created by spring sunshine, he noted, 'Thus it seemed that this one hillside illustrated the principle of all the operations of Nature. The Maker of this Earth but patented a leaf.'

A Creative Future

Unlike those of us who spend too much time caught up in and distracted by the noise of the town, Thoreau is alert to the sound of birdsong. In the case of the grackle, he notes an imperfection in nature and optimistically looks for an improvement! 'I saw some blackbirds, apparently grackles, singing, after their fashion, on a tree by the river... They were pruning themselves and splitting their throats in vain, trying to sing... All the melody flew off in splinters.' ... 'Yet, as *nature is a becoming*, their notes may become melodious at last.' I love this sense he has of nature being a developing process, open-ended, not yet finished. The world, as he sees it, has a creative future; and that thought lifts my heart.

Sound and Silence

Thoreau shows much greater respect for the owl than he does for the grackle, even when sometimes finding its hooting full of melancholy and foreboding. He reflects on how much harder the owl is to see than it is to hear, and will walk miles to listen to its calling. In the silence of a night-time wood, the solitary hoot of an owl awakens the listener to whole volumes of space not appreciated before. It creates in the silence a great cathedral of depth and height between the trunks of the forest. 'They give me a new sense of the vastness and mystery of that nature which is the common dwelling of us both.'

I find in these reflections, on the hooting of owls in the night, an important thought about the interplay between sound and silence; that they depend upon and enhance each other. We can never seek silence on its own without sound; in the natural world, sound and silence come together.

SILENCE IN THE SONG OF THE NIGHTINGALE

◆

Most human activity generates noise, whether we are travelling to work, cooking a meal or building a house; even before machinery became part of the domestic scene, our creative lives were full of noisy clatter and conversation. But the natural organic world is different; a great oak tree grows in silence.

IT IS ONE OF THE MYSTERIES OF THE WORLD we inhabit that beauty emerges silently from the soil. We only have to stand and stare in a spring garden or by a hedgerow to appreciate that fact; fresh leaves unfurl from winter twigs; cow parsley froths along the bank; tulips emerge from bulbs in the ground and bloom in the breeze. We do nothing – it just happens around us.

It is true too of birdsong. The poet Tennyson contemplated this mystery when wondering about the singing of one of our most melodious northern migrants who sings in the dark. Where does the glorious song come from?

◆

'Lay hidden, as the music of the moon
Sleeps in the plain eggs of the nightingale.'

◆

Announcing the Coming of Spring

Michael McCarthy bears witness to the relationship between sound and silence when contemplating the song of the nightingale, in his book *Say Goodbye to the Cuckoo*. He writes about one of the wonders of the natural world, the yearly migration of sixteen million birds up from sub-Saharan Africa to the woodlands and hedgerows of Britain. They are part of our folklore and history, announcing the coming of spring and raising our spirits. Sadly, many of our favourite migrants – the swallow, wood warbler, nightingale and cuckoo – are dwindling in numbers, owing to changes in agricultural practice, global warming and drought in the southern hemisphere. In *Say Goodbye to the Cuckoo*, McCarthy spends a spring season locating, seeing and listening to them all, and wondering if there is anything we can do about the decline of these birds.

A Duet with Silence

He is guided by a friend to a spot where he can listen to the nightingale singing in the dark in an untamed part of Surrey. Here, with a sense of wonder, he discovers the interplay of sound and silence, and in particular the role of silence in the nightingale's song. 'With open eyes I could see nothing. I could hear nothing else. All that there was in existence was this song, and I realised then that it was a duet with silence. Silence was its background; silence moulded it, silence made it perfect, as it filled the world entirely.'

SEEKING SILENCE IN NATURE

◆

*We do not have to go far to find a place where we can find silence in
Nature. It is not necessary to follow in the footsteps of Thoreau and
retreat to a hermitage for years. All we have to do is to take a walk
and when we come to some woodland, a grove, an open field, or a
hedgerow, to stop and listen.*

S OME OF THE SIGNS OF SILENCE are visual and not heard.
I do not have to walk far from my home in East Sussex to
be on the banks of the meandering Cuckmere River where it
runs between the South Downs. On a spring day, it is not long
before I see a heron.

A fishing heron is an object lesson in patience and silence.
It stands in absorbed and focused stillness. With reeds about
it, legs lost in the wet grass, the heron stands unmoving for
longer than we might care to watch. Its gaze runs down the
lethal spear of its bill, eyeing a frog, a fish or a tadpole.
A cautious step forward is followed by more stillness. This, I
feel, is how we should observe the things of nature – absorbed,
silent, with only our breathing shaping the stillness.

From Stillness to Stillness

I now look for silence in the behaviour of other birds and
animals wherever I go; it can be found among the smallest and
the largest of creatures.

I was staying in northern Kenya, and one evening made my way out of the bush and up on to a piece of open high grassland. Some impala saw me and sped away, 'pronking' over thorn bushes with magic ability, a show of leaping fitness to distract my attention from their young ones. But it was a pair of tiny plovers no bigger than sparrows that most entertained me. Unlike the foraging of some birds such as warblers, who are busy all the time flitting from branch to branch, calling to each other in active agitation, the plovers stood totally still in silence, focused on the ground ahead of them. Suddenly they would move a few feet and take up a new silent vigil. They scuttled from stillness to stillness.

Silent Elephants

At the other end of the scale of size, I was surprised to discover how unexpectedly silent elephants can be. I was sitting by the last burning embers of a fire. The blue moonlit landscape of leleshwa sage bush spread undulating to the horizon; the Moon and the burning sticks the only light visible in any direction. I noticed a movement out in the bush and watched entranced as a troupe of elephants quietly made their way along a bleached grass track between the acacias. They seemed so big, with their little ones running alongside like miniature adults. The elephants were great blue shadows the size of trees; as big as houses. Who would have thought that such a massive animal as an elephant could walk so silently?

AN APPOINTMENT WITH A TREE

◆

The Indian poet Tagore once wrote, 'Be still then, for each tree is a silent prayer.' There is even a folk tradition in India that trees are the reincarnations of philosophers, who after a lifetime of thinking need a break from philosophy to enjoy just 'being' in silence.

B Y THE STILLNESS OF A TREE we can find a great place to meditate in silence, particularly a tree that was there before we were born. Trees have a timeless, silent presence, which is worth getting to know. We do ourselves a favour if we are able to identify one or two trees that we can make minor pilgrimages to now and then, to get to know them, link up with their peace. Thoreau even records walking ten miles through the snow one winter to keep an appointment with a beech tree. He doesn't say why, but just refers to the event as though it were the most natural thing in the world.

Communing with Trees

Thoreau was a great reader and he always enjoyed a serious conversation with a well-read neighbour. Yet there were times when he preferred the company of a tree, writing: 'Instead of calling on some scholar, I paid many a visit to particular trees, of a kind which are rare in this neighbourhood, standing far away in the middle of some pasture, or in the depths of a wood or swamp, or on a hill-top…'

There are many trees I have an old fondness for, both in town and country. I love to stand beneath them, stroke their boles, gaze up into their branches. One of these is an old oak tree standing in a small field by a drystone wall in Wasdale, Cumbria. Wasdale is a moist valley and green moss clings to the trunk all around and not just on the north side away from the drying sunshine. The trunk is bold and thick with a twist to it as it rises upward before spreading out in many great limbs; its bark is rough and fissured, like the skin of an ancient mammoth. The sweet coconut smell of yellow gorse drifts down on the warm air from a low knoll in the next field; old brittle bracken crunches underfoot. Ancient stone walls by the old bridle track have become banks where blue-bell and wood sorrel grow.

A Visit to the Oak

I visited the oak this spring, as I have done around Easter for many years. I find the ancientness of the tree and the newness of spring make a wonderful combination, a living symbol of hope, renewal, and resurrection from darker days. While the leaves are still tight little fists of yellow freshness, beginning to unwrap in the sunshine, a redstart, newly arrived from Africa with the spring migration, hawks for insects in the canopy. Flicking his russet tail gently, he repeats his subdued throaty call and I am aware that winter is over. I know no better silence than in the stillness of that great oak tree.

A Forest Meditation

◆

It can be a good thing to enter some woodland or forest or jungle, on your own, to find a place to stop, and if possible to sit awhile, to contemplate mindfully all that you see around you, and then to consider that you too are part of the rich organic scene.

OUR FAMILIAR WORD 'JUNGLE', with all its rich connotations of biodiversity and wildness, comes down to us from Sanskrit, one of the oldest recorded languages on Earth. Forests and jungles have surrounded us for the whole of human history, formative powers in our experience of the world. They are part of our psyche and figure prominently in myth and legend, fairytale and folklore. Hansel and Gretel are not the only ones to have been terrified at the thought of being lost deep in the woods.

Forest Bathing

Some people find forests scary, and would not feel at all at home wandering in one on their own. It is a natural fear but well worth overcoming, because the experience of walking in a wood can be wonderful. Many national parks now have well-marked forest tracks where even the most wary can venture safely. At first, for the fearful, it could be done in the company of a friend; later, with confidence, a short stroll into the edge of a forest alone can be attempted. The effort will be worth it.

In fact, it seems that spending time in a forest can be physically good for us. Japanese researchers have found that two to three days spent holidaying in a forest boosts the human immune system. The equivalent time spent as a tourist in a city or at a leisure centre does not have the same effect. The practice is called 'Shinrin-yoku' – 'forest bathing'. The theory is that by immersing oneself in a forest (bathing in its atmosphere, soaking it up) we expose ourselves to airborne chemicals that plants release to protect themselves against rotting and insects. Bless the trees!

At One with the Forest

Imagine you are part of the forest, as you sit a moment looking about and listening. This can become a positive, mindful meditation. Try to dig deep into the thought that all of nature is one evolving web of life. We human beings do not stand outside it – we are part of it, one of the many branches of the rich jungle of biodiversity that covers the surface of the Earth. When we look at the forest, we are scrutinizing an extension of ourselves – or seeing ourselves as an extension of the forest. This is where we belong.

I came across this idea of practising a meditation on being part of the forest in one of the world's best-managed national parks, the Mount Field National Park in Tasmania. Some of the tallest eucalypts in Australia grow on the slopes of Mount Field; massive swamp gums (sometimes called mountain ash)

'Stop for a moment and imagine you are part of the forest.'

soar almost 100 metres (300 feet) above the tree ferns and myrtle down on the forest floor. Yellow-crested white cockatoos screech high in the canopy while scarlet robins flit across the path from moss pile to fallen log. Waterfalls add to the lushness. It is an atmospheric place.

It was an imaginative notice by a well-placed seat that caught my attention. 'Stop for a moment and imagine you are part of the forest,' it suggested. Here was a thought worth pursuing, I reflected, gazing around at the giant tree trunks.

Our Extended Family

Tracing the family tree has become a popular activity recently, particularly with the internet making it so easy. Very quickly the simple tree becomes an elaborate bush of connections sharing sap with other equally dense and branching bushes. Imagine if we could trace our personal ancestry back through history, through the mammal line, through amphibians to fishes and beyond. Such a line surely exists, or we would not be here (though, as we found with the bush metaphor, there will be many alternative lines of descent, all equally true). Eventually the line of forebears – whichever one we choose to focus on – will take us back to a period of history one

billion years ago when we find ourselves sharing ancestors
with the tree we contemplate in the forest.

Distant Cousins

The trees are our very distant cousins. Some of our DNA is
still the same. The trees have followed a different lineage from
us, as have the mosses, the toadstools and the birds flitting
through the canopy, but we are nevertheless related. We are
cousins, too, to all the flowers, to the grass in the meadow and
to the wheat from which we bake our daily bread. What better
place to absorb and digest these truths than in the silence of
a woodland walk?

Sharing Roots

Twenty or so years ago a fascinating article by Ernest Kurtz
was brought to my notice by a pupil; it made a similar point
about our shared origins with the rest of nature, but through
linguistics. Two common words in English stem from the
same Indo-European root, 'ghom': *human* and *humus*. Look
again at the rich compost on the forest floor, the crumbling
leaves, the rotting wood, the rich-smelling loam of vegetation
being broken down by bacteria, fungus and insect – '*humus*'.
Great for the garden, we think. But our own growth is dependent on vegetation and we share kinship as much with the soil
as we do with the trees, the grass and the wheat. We are, as it
were, just animated bits of the ground.

THE TREE AS A COUNSELLOR

The phrase 'touch wood' unconsciously acknowledges an ancient and deep veneration for trees. Some modern Druids have revived this religious respect for trees, and even developed a technique for using a tree as a silent counsellor to whom one can unburden one's troubles.

I CAME ACROSS THIS PRACTICE OF TALKING to trees when addressing a conference of science teachers in a rural hotel down in Dorset. Half the hotel was occupied by scientists, and half by Druids. An interesting combination! The Druids would conduct their meetings out in the open, standing in circles in fields. Sometimes they disappeared individually into the woods – and the rest of us were intrigued. In conversation over dinner we shared our various interests, and it was then that I learnt about tree hugging, and taking a tree into your confidence. Now this was going a bit too far for comfort from my own tradition, whether as a priest or as a scientist. But it seemed harmless and the people commending it very charming and straightforward, so I decided to give it a go. In fact, many of us did from the science group.

The Druids would conduct their meetings out in the open, standing in circles in fields.

I walked off into the woods feeling, I have to admit, mildly silly. A bit of investigation and a certain amount of wandering rather aimlessly around brought me to the foot of a large, smooth-trunked beech tree, well out of earshot of anyone else (I checked extremely carefully!).

May I Talk to You?

You are instructed to ask the tree for its permission to use it as a counsellor, after walking around its base three times clockwise, keeping the tree on your right. I pushed my way through some young saplings and over the odd log and root as I made my circumambulations, then stopped. 'May I talk to you?' I asked tentatively.

Looking up through the branches – it was still early spring – I saw a buzzard circling the top of the tree on a thermal, turning in the same direction as I had just walked. I took that to be a 'Yes'. So I knew I was going to be here for an hour, posing various questions to the tree while sitting at its base facing, east, west, north then south. Who am I? Where have I come from? Where am I going? What should I now do?

The tree was silent and the hour was actually very fruitful. There *were* some issues I needed to sort out, when I came to think about it. The uninterrupted silence (thankfully none of my conference companions hit on the same tree!) and the beautiful setting were very conducive to thought. When I was asking, 'Where am I going?', my attention focused on a fresh bud hanging down close to my face. It was beginning to unfurl into deliciously fresh new life. I found it a surprisingly helpful image and very apposite at the time.

THE STILLNESS & SILENCE OF ROCKS

Great rocks have their own weight and silent presence, resting, perhaps for many millennia, in one spot. Anyone who has stood among the towering formations in Monument Valley in Utah, USA, or at the foot of Uluru in the Red Centre of Australia knows this — the gravity of their silence is immense.

THE STILLNESS OF A ROCK is archetypal and literally monolithic. Standing stones — whether in small stone circles erected in pre-Celtic days on the moors of Cumbria, or in the great henges that can be seen in the northern Isles of Orkney or on the Salisbury plain — have always fascinated us. Even a simple monolith, standing alone in a field, holds a silent mystery, a silent history.

One of my favourite rocks has a name — 'The Dwarfie Stone'; it rests on the heath in the heather of a valley beneath a cliff called the Dwarfie Hamars, on the Orkney Island of Hoy. This great boulder fell from the hill above probably at the end of the last Ice Age. Five thousand years ago it was hollowed out as a double burial chamber; today it is empty and one can crawl inside the tomb through a low square entrance. The silence and stillness is palpable and is not disturbed even when the wind whistles down the valley through the heather, and a curlew cries overhead.

A Charitable 'Mynde'

I am reminded, when thinking of the Dwarfie Stone, of a line from the sixteenth-century humanist Thomas Lupset: 'No rocke is more style, than is the mynde of a charitable man' (he wrote at a time when spelling was different and personal variations didn't matter!). Lupset highlights an important truth by suggesting that none of us can achieve an inner stillness and silence if we do not also develop a right and proper attitude to our fellow human beings. This truth is encapsulated in the Judeo-Christian commandment to 'Love your neighbour as yourself'; in Buddhism it is enshrined in the Eightfold Path as 'Right Speech', Right Action' and 'Right Livelihood'. Silence without a life of kindness can never be truly restful.

'It is a solemn awful place. As I entered the charmed circle of the sombre Stones I instinctively uncovered my head. It was like entering a great Cathedral Church.

A great silent service was going on and the Stones inaudibly whispered to each other the grand secret.'

REV. KILVERT ON VISITING STONEHENGE IN 1875, FROM 'KILVERT'S DIARY'
JONATHAN CAPE, 1960

Silent Night & the Stars

◆

A short walk in the dark before going to bed can be a very restful thing. Above the turmoil of the world, beyond the clouds, the Moon and stars drift silently across the sky; contemplating them can relax our being into a more peaceful state of mind.

I T HELPS TO KNOW THE CONSTELLATIONS, to be able to repeat their names and the names of the stars within them. Getting to know the night sky is simpler than it sometimes seems and very rewarding; the stars are always there, and only the Moon and planets change their positions as you become familiar with the shapes of the constellations. Many of their names are ancient – Orion and the Pleiades, Ursa Major the Great Bear, and Cygnus the Swan. Contemplating them in silence can be a great balm after a noisy day.

The Sound of Starlight

In actual fact the stars in themselves are not silent; they are gigantic furnaces of restrained power, generating nuclear energy in quantities that defy imagination. No wind-tossed sea on Earth, however titanic the storm, could even begin to match one-thousandth of the turmoil that disturbs the surface of a star; the waves of heat that rip through the incandescent gases of its atmosphere; the geysers of energy that flare up hundreds of thousands of miles, trumpeting in decibels of thunder that would shatter our ears and shake our beings to bits if we were there. We know all this because we now have intimate knowledge of our own nearest star, the Sun.

The stars roar. The waves of sound that beat across their surfaces are deeper than the cathedral-shaking vibrations of the largest *basso profundo* organ pipe ever devised or imagined by man. But we don't hear them, because they are so far away and because interstellar space is virtually empty and so sound waves cannot reach us. Distance (as sometimes between people!) lends its own peace and silence.

VISION SEEKERS AMONG THE NATIVE AMERICANS

◆

It has long been a tradition among young men (and, to a lesser extent, young women) descended from the pre-Columbian tribes of North America to seek life guidance out in the wilderness, away from other people. Alone in the silence of the forest, they consult the spirits of nature, who send dreams to them, and visions.

LATER THESE DREAMS ARE INTERPRETED by a shaman or village elder and in this way they discover their adult name and the role they are destined to play in community life. They might be guided to become a tracker or a warrior, or, if plants and herbs figured in their dreams, a medicine man.

The experience of growing up has been marked by cere-mony throughout history and adult initiation rituals are a common feature of almost all societies. These ceremonies are one of the important 'rites of passage' that mark a significant watershed in a person's life. They have often been challenging, frightening, and a test of survival. In our modern society they have become much tamer – a confirmation at school or in a local church, or a Bar Mitzvah.

The Vision-seeking Ritual

The details differ from tribe to tribe, from Sioux to Paiute to Ojibway, but they all follow a similar pattern. Frequently a sauna bath is involved, in a low dwelling of branches covered with sods built especially for the purpose. Stones heated in a fire are placed inside and water thrown over them. This is the cleansing the young initiate needs before setting off on his lonely journey as a vision seeker. His father may accompany him to the forest and help him dig a vision pit at the foot of a tree, a small hollow in the ground covered with branches. He will then be left alone, perhaps naked, to face the silence in solitude, for three days or even a week.

Dreams of the Future

The fears are real – wolf, bear and mountain lion share the same forest. And there is the problem of finding food. In some rites a pipe is left for the initiate, with tobacco to help bring on visions. Night-time dreams and daytime visions (perhaps induced by sleeplessness, smoking, adolescent fear and also expectation) become very real in the boy's experience. They are the material that will guide a wise elder, later, to find a name for the boy – 'Running Deer' or 'Sitting Bull'. He will also discover through these dreams whether he is to be a tracker, medicine man, or warrior (and hopefully not to be the 'heyoka', a man blessed with sacred power but doomed to spend his life as the village fool doing everything the wrong way round, from riding a horse to answering questions, saying yes for no and vice versa). The dreams will determine, too, the contents of his medicine bundle, a small bag of objects he will wear round his neck as a protective talisman.

The Original Hiawatha

When you live in a culture that takes dreams and visions so seriously, and you live in expectation of having them, it is not surprising that a boy left on his own in the wild will have strange stories to tell of things he has heard and seen.

Some visions from the adult initiation rite have entered the stream of public storytelling and become famous. One such is the Legend of Mondawmin, upon which the poet Longfellow based his story of Hiawatha. The original character was Wunzh, an Ojibway Indian of the Great Lakes region.

Wunzh's Story

Wunzh comes from a poor family, starving as the father has had little success from hunting. The boy retreats to the woods for a week-long fast, hoping that through vision he will get some idea about how better to feed his hungry family. For a couple of days he wanders about the mountains and forests examining plants and flowers and wondering which might be good to eat. Each night he returns to the small bivouac that has been built for him. On the third day he is too tired and faint from hunger to walk, and lies listlessly on his bed. This is when his visions begin.

A young warrior gaily clad in green and yellow with a great plume of feathers on his head descends from the clouds, claiming to have been sent by the Wakan Tanka, the Great Spirit, and challenges him to a friendly fight. This is repeated day after day until the final day of his fast, when the warrior from the sky instructs him to fight again, but this time they must struggle to the death; Wunzh is to kill his new friend. Having killed him, he is to clear some ground by his bivouac and bury the body. Thereafter he is to return to the spot regularly and keep the ground clear of weeds and grass.

Happy Ending

Wunzh faithfully obeys the instructions of his sky friend. Cleared of weeds, a fresh blade appears from the ground and grows. Come the autumn, it has become a tall and healthy plant, green and yellow with plumes on great husks of corn.

'It is my friend Mondawmin [maize],' cries the boy. 'He has returned.' The family is fed and the tribe become successful farmers rather than hopeless hunters. One cannot help but note the creative usefulness of this legend, recounting a piece of social history; and the respect it shows for the practical consequences of time spent alone in silence.

Facing Yourself in Silence

Several organizations today offer to help teenagers of any race or religion in America to experience the adult initiation ceremony for themselves; to retreat to a wilderness place for a couple of days and taste the solitude. The emphasis is not so much on dreams or visions but in facing yourself in silence; having a chance to discover a bit more about who you are; growing up. One couple I heard of spent three days in Death Valley. They camped in separate locations and twice a day added a stone to a cairn to indicate that they were fine.

A third person checked the cairns regularly. I have driven through Death Valley. It is an oven and only a grackle could sing its splintered song from a dry bit of scrub. I love the heat but I think that that would be *too* much for me; to my mind it would stifle the silence.

> *The emphasis is not so much on dreams or visions but in facing yourself in silence.*

CHAPTER FIVE

THE STRANGE ATTRACTION OF THE MONASTERY

*Ever since the Desert Fathers retreated to
live alone in the Egyptian desert, there have been
Christians who have felt called to a life of silence behind
the walls of a monastery. Hundreds of years earlier, monks
and nuns following the teachings of the Buddha had
responded to the same need to congregate and to meditate.
If we are to understand ourselves better, we may find it
helpful to meditate on why so many have felt attracted to
this way of life, particularly those drawn to live a life of
total silence. Monasticism has something important to
tell us about the nature of our humanity.*

A TIME TO KEEP SILENCE

◆

To every thing there is a season,
and a time to every purpose under the heaven…
a time to keep silence, and a time to speak…

FROM ECCLESIASTES 3

◆

For most of us, it is enough to learn how to locate the pauses in the noise and bustle of daily life in our modern world, to stop activity for those still moments and cherish them. Others, however, are drawn further and deeper into their search for peace and silence.

THERE ARE MANY WHO WILLINGLY, and with some eager anticipation, seek the discipline of a monastic way of life, not as an escape from the world or from the responsibilities of life, but as a positive move towards a more conscious and aware mode of living. They see it, in fact, as a step *up* in life.

The well-known travel writer Patrick Leigh Fermor also wrote about an inner journey he made when he stayed in some of Europe's oldest and most venerable monasteries. Quoting the line above from Ecclesiastes, he called his delightful yet short book *A Time to Keep Silence*.

The Seclusion of a Cell

He was profoundly affected by his sojourns in these ancient monasteries, and he writes in the introduction about the

discovery of silence and solitude. 'For in the seclusion of a cell
– an existence whose quietness is only varied by the silent
meals, the solemnity of ritual and long solitary walks in the
woods – the troubled waters of the mind grow still and clear,
and much that is hidden away and all that clouds it floats to the
surface and can be skimmed away; after a time one reaches a
state of peace that is unthought-of in the ordinary world.'

I very much admire Leigh Fermor's perseverance in seeking to understand the monastic life. I had less success myself
when I was young. The experience at theological college
referred to in an earlier chapter left me mostly untouched
and I felt urged to explore further. I wrote to the abbot of one
of our most famous Roman Catholic monasteries and asked if
I might stay for a week or two in return for doing some work
in the kitchens. 'No need to work in the kitchens,' the kindly
abbot wrote back, 'just come as a guest.'

Monastic Sojourn

I was cordially greeted by the guest-master, who showed me
to where I was to stay; not so much a cell as a small clean
room with bed, table and chair. Instructions about the fire
escape were pasted to the back of the door and the window
looked out onto a building full of other anonymous windows.
It was a big institution. He gave me a timetable for collegiate
meals and for the various daily offices in chapel, showed me
the refectory, cloisters and garden, and then quietly left me to

my own devices. The monastery had an air of purposeful activity and the chapel smelt of incense.

I could not settle and wanted to get away and move on. My attempt at a plan of activity by offering my services in the kitchens had been thwarted. Monastic life is usually a mixture of hard physical work, in the gardens perhaps, interspersed with prayer, sleep and study. I had brought several books with me to study but I had no work. I needed some physical toil to give my mind a rest. As it was, I was left feeling fidgety, and discovered no inner silence.

Not For Me...

It soon became apparent that I had stumbled into the same mistake I had made when heading off for a week on my own to a cottage on Birker Moor to 'do some writing' – going on a retreat without any clear objective in mind. The monks went about their daily business and I was clearly welcome but I felt an alien. The 'What am I doing here?' question afflicted me again. This was not the life for me. I did not have the necessary patience or dedication; I survived a few days and left.

I never did find silence through the cloister. Others can and do. For me the experience of solitude and silence has always been part of the natural world, a glorious discovery found through mindful walking and meditation; through getting to know the surface of the Moon and contemplating the stars; and through patiently observing the behaviour of birds.

Leigh Fermor's Retreat

Leigh Fermor had the sensible advantage of having a positive plan and purpose that kept him in the monastery during the first difficult days – he had a book to write. His retreat took him from a busy life of late-night drinking with a circle of friends in Paris to a quiet beech-wooded valley in Normandy and the Abbey of St Wandrille de Fontanelle. St Wandrille is inhabited by a Benedictine community and has been a place of prayer and silence since the seventh century; a history of the abbey could trace the history of France for well over a thousand years, through war and revolution, enlightenment and reformation; through days of power (when the abbey owned property and parishes in England) and days of destruction. St Wandrille's magnificent ruins are known to the thousands of tourists who pass by each year, buying honey or shoe polish (hard and traditional) from the community shop. What the tourists do not see is the calm and ordered life of silent monks as they quietly go about their prayerful business, close-by but remote beyond the high walls. It is another world.

Finding Peace

The first days of Leigh Fermor's retreat were painful – the sudden contrast with his sociable drinking life in Paris meant that his initial experience was of extreme loneliness and boredom. He lay awake at night, felt tired by day, and found the times in chapel tedious. But he broke through this barrier and then found himself overcome by prodigious hours of deep sleep that astonished him; it was as though all the anxieties and tensions of his earlier life were catching up with him. It was only after all of this that his body and mind were able to adjust to the new tempo of the abbey and he began to find the peace in his cell that he describes in *A Time to Keep Silence*.

Total Silence

Later in his travels, Leigh Fermor visited the austere monastery of La Grande Trappe, mother ship of the Trappist Order, which is the loose and general term for the Cistercian order of the Strict Observance. The silence is virtually total.

⌁ Into Great Silence ⌁

Some readers will be familiar with Philip Gröning's film of 2005, *Into Great Silence*. This exquisitely beautiful and slow-moving documentary reveals something of the silent life of a monk while at prayer or working in the garden of the Grande Chartreuse, the head monastery of another contemplative religious order (the Carthusian) in the French Alps. The silence is less absolute than at La Grande Trappe but the pace of life there can be gauged from the fact it took Gröning sixteen years, from his first letter to the general prior, to be granted permission to film behind the monastery walls!

ELECTED SILENCE

It is an irony of the religious life that it was a Trappist monastery, Gethsemani in Kentucky (founded on the principles of La Grande Trappe, but somewhat more relaxed in its ways), that produced one of the great religious writers and communicators of the twentieth century, Thomas Merton.

MERTON WAS AN ADMIRED CONTEMPORARY of my father and his book *Elected Silence* held a prominent place on the bookshelf in his study. Another copy adorns my own bookshelf. *Elected Silence* is an English version of the hugely popular *The Seven Storey Mountain*; its publication inspired many young men to follow Merton to Gethsemani and other monasteries; he had become in effect, and unwittingly, a recruiting sergeant for the silent life.

A Contemplative Life

Merton had had a somewhat troubled and turbulent life as a child and later as a young man, but had a deep yearning within him from very early on for the disciplined life of a silent contemplative. He records that while still at elementary school he found a picture in a volume of religious architecture of the Carthusian monastery La Grande Chartreuse: 'My heart was filled with a kind of longing to breathe the air of that lonely valley and listen to its silence.'

For a Trappist to become an author was quite a remarkable break with tradition; unlike some other contemplative orders, the Cistercian rule of the Trappists left little time for private study or contemplation – it was an austere life of hard physical work and prayer, with virtually no private space and lived almost always in the presence of other monks.

By Sign & Gesture

Communication happened, of course, but unless it was in conversation with your confessor or on important community business it had to be by sign and gesture. Merton records that over four hundred hand signs were used at Gethsemani, including a large vocabulary of joke signs – including one for 'Drop dead'. The silent life is not without its humour!

The popularity of *Elected Silence* revealed the tremendous human need for peace and stillness, particularly after a period of war. After the Second World War, when the Cold War had begun to take a grip on nations, many war veterans sought refuge in the monasteries of the contemplative orders. They sought peace in the silent discipline of a monastic life.

We crave to find that still point in our turning world. Merton's fame spread and he became a hero of the spiritual life, illustrating with renewed clarity that paradox highlighted by Peter France in his book *Hermits: The Insights of Solitude* – that the world will beat a path to the door of a person who has retreated from society.

SILENCE AS A UNIFIER

◆

One of the fruits of silent contemplation, I profoundly believe, is the discovery of a deep unity between the religions of the world. We can then face the doctrinal differences with greater understanding and respect. In a world fractured by hatred and mistrust, shared silence becomes the great Unifier.

TOO OFTEN IT IS THE DOCTRINAL EXTREMISTS who grab the headlines; the scriptural fundamentalists in Christian tradition proclaiming that only they hold the truth and that all other religions are from the Devil; the jihadists of Islam mesmerized by martyrdom. Every religion, it seems, has its bigoted wing stuck with the view that only they are right.

Yet one of the truly hopeful signs in the growing pains of our global economy is the rise of the Interfaith Movement since the end of the nineteenth century. In 1873 a World Parliament of Religions, the first of its kind, convened in Chicago. It signalled the beginning of a healing process.

Merton at Large

Thomas Merton was one who from the silence of his monastery began a creative and searching dialogue with eastern religious spirituality, with Buddhism, Hinduism and Taoism. His writings became very well known, his correspondence immense (more letters pouring into his cell than for all the other monks put together), and eventually he was allowed to travel as a sort of PR man for the Trappist tradition – an incongruous situation to find himself in.

Bare Attention

He became deeply attracted to the Zen Buddhist tradition, with its emphasis on 'seeing' the way things are in the here and now. He produced a lovely book, *Zen and the Birds of Appetite*, in which he writes about the importance of 'mindfulness' in the Buddhist tradition. 'Buddhist "mindfulness" or awareness ... in its most elementary form consists in that 'bare attention' which simply sees what is right there and does not add any comment, any interpretation, any judgement, any conclusion. It just sees. Learning to see in this manner is the basic and fundamental exercise of Buddhist meditation.'

A Common Quest

Merton found great friendship with monks of other traditions, Tibetan and Zen Buddhist; they discovered a common language together and shared deep down the same spiritual quest. They laughed a lot and some of his new colleagues took the view that he was a 'natural Buddha'. I can understand well how this might be so. When studying for an MA at Lancaster University, there were half a dozen saffron-clad Buddhist monks on the same course, attending the same tutorials. What struck me most about these fellow students was that after only a few weeks we ceased to think of them as *Buddhist* monks; they were just monks, living a quiet and disciplined life, familiar with meditation and silence.

Perhaps this is the way forward for the religions of the world; to encourage the growing mindful awareness that we are one human race, pursuing a fragile and precarious existence. Instead of stirring up wars, religion could become the great unifier. We share the same spiritual quest, whatever our culture or language, and deep down in the silence there is a real chance that we might at last find one human faith.

Snowflakes Drifting...

Years ago I read a Zen Buddhist haiku which impressed me with its simple essence. The Zen haiku helps both the composer of the poem, and also the reader, see things as they are; they encourage a mindful awareness of the reality of the present moment. I can no longer locate where I came across this haiku or even accurately recall the exact words, so I have had to reconstruct it. It was an image of silence.

Snowflakes drifting

From the sky settle gently

In a silver bowl.

I often stop what I am doing and let this image settle gently into my mind.

CHAPTER SIX

HANDLING NOISE

We cannot, except in our dreams, say 'Stop the world — I want to get off'! In the twenty-first century, human society has to face many challenging problems, all of which, with a will, could be solved if there were cooperation and mutual respect between people. Less pressing, perhaps, than some of the major ills facing millions of our fellow citizens is the growth of noise pollution. What can we do about it? And if we can't change it, and can't escape it, then how do we live with it?

SENSITIVITY TO NOISE

Each of us are tolerant of different amounts and levels of noise, even at home. Some can work with music playing loudly; others find it impossible to concentrate even if the radio is playing in another room; some keep the TV on for company; others hate its presence unless they are watching it.

S OME OF US ARE ACTUALLY PHYSICALLY MORE SENSITIVE to noise. I once ran a swimming club for autistic children in our school pool and discovered that although these little characters were hopeless at communication (throw one a ball, he'd catch it then just throw it away with no more interest in you; talk to another and he would stare straight through you and take no notice of anything you said), they reacted severely to noise. If one screamed, others would push their fingers in their ears and run in distress to the far end of the building. A favourite trick of one autistic teenager was to quietly sink beneath the water if the noise levels rose. The soundless peace of the underwater world must have been soothing for him. He always came up laughing, while we kept a slightly anxious watch over his safety.

A Sliding Scale of Silence

I suspect we are all on a spectrum of sensitivity, which means that our definitions of silence will be on a sliding scale. Our toleration or appreciation of silence is also on a sliding scale and in some respects is age-related. Today, I love and cherish almost any amount of silence, but when I was a child silence could weigh heavily, particularly in school holidays. Who has not stood as a child, staring out of the window at cold grey rain, complaining, 'Mum – I've got nothing to do!'

Silence can be such an exciting place, as we may be lucky enough to discover as we get older. Anyone wishing to get to know it should treat themselves to a retreat as a starter. It doesn't have to be 'churchy', although there are many excellent religious retreat houses and if a formal retreat with a retreat master is one's inclination then they are worth investigating. If you prefer to be on your own, then a week or weekend in a country cottage could be a good way to begin (rent for a week and then have someone join you after the weekend?). Don't, at first, be over ambitious.

Remote Silence

The Iona Community, referred to in an earlier chapter, rent out cottages for groups or individuals (see their well-designed website). One centre, called Camas, on Mull has a wonderful mission statement: 'Together we seek to enable growth in love, respect and awareness of ourselves, each other, God and the environment.' I can't think of a better definition of the purpose of seeking silence. Between autumn and spring (off season) you could plan for yourself a self-catering retreat at

Camas in a remote cottage between the rocks and the sea and be as alone as you like. But remember, unless you already know yourself very well, learn from my early mistakes. Have a plan and purpose for each day – never allow yourself to slump into that lonely question, 'What am I doing here?'

Mindful Retreat

I have myself led the occasional group retreat for church people and have always guided the group to go out for walks and become aware of the living environment around them; to have a personal quest to observe and notice. It could be as simple as looking for different types of moss! – or getting to recognize the way the limbs grow on different trees. That world we take for granted, the natural environment, has its own life – it is 'other'; it is not just a background to the busy life of people. I find it works as a good theme for a retreat.

If you like the idea of a retreat, then do some research, ask around, and find who recommends what and why. There are many opportunities, Christian, Buddhist, Hindu or secular. Looking for the right retreat for yourself is part of the process that will help prepare you for the experience.

Become aware of the living environment.

FINDING SILENCE IN THE CHACO

◆

After several attempts in my life, I have found the way to spend a joyful week or more in solitude and silence — I need a purpose and a project, something that will give a structure to my time alone. I suspect that this will be true for most people.

I SPENT TEN DAYS ON MY OWN IN PARAGUAY quite recently. I didn't even think of it as a retreat as such, but the silence and solitude were glorious. And I had a project, which held it together. I had learnt from my past mistakes!

I have a slim volume on my shelf that has been with me for well over half a century — a King Penguin book, *Birds of La Plata*. It contains sixteen colour plates of such marvels as the crested cardinal and the glittering hummingbird; the blue and yellow tanager and the scarlet tyrant; the firewood-gatherer and the southern crested screamer. My project was to see all these birds and sketch them as a basis for some paintings. Friends have a ranch some miles north of Asunción and they were happy for me to stay there while they were visiting Chile. Ten days of not having to talk to anyone, except to myself; that is what silence means to me. Wonderful.

Peace Before the Storm

Those days in silence passed joyfully. I saw all the birds I was looking for and many more; sketchbook and journal kept me occupied. I walked every day marvelling at the violet water hyacinths by the tracks, the caiman alligators in the swamp; the hedgehog-sized armadillo that scuttled across my path. I often had time to sit on the veranda, watch the sunset and wait there while day turned through twilight into night, bats replacing birds in the darkening sky.

The pampas savannah of the Chaco is hot and silent during the day, apart from the occasional call of a bird and the odd breeze stirring the dry grass or rustling the brittle dead palm leaves. But one afternoon heavy black cumulus clouds began to gather, the air became oppressively hot and humid, and thunder started to roll around the horizon. All sounds of birds ceased. Everything was waiting in silence for the storm.

The Storm Breaks...

When the rain came it was with a roar, flooding from the sky in torrents. I stood in the doorway of the ranch house, relieved at the cooling sound, and watched. And the birds! I had thought the birds would go for cover. No such thing. The ovenbirds and the great kiskadee flycatchers positively applauded! They perched in the trees and vied with the rain to be heard, with whoops and whistles and raucous cheers. Their delight was infectious and made me roar with laughter and cheer with them.

The rain stopped, the noise subsided to a gurgling of drain-pipes from the rooftops, and the birds calmed down from their ecstatic celebrations. The sky cleared and I watched through a glorious sunset as the day settled into a quiet evening. Or so I thought. It was quiet for a time as darkness fell. The stars came out, Alpha Centauri and the Southern Cross ablaze in the sort of velvet black sky we no longer see in England. Fireflies started to drift through the branches of the trees as though some of the stars were on the move, changing constellation for constellation. It was all silence and peace.

A Glorious Cacophony

And then the noise began. The cicadas introduced the concert; a wave of swelling sound swept across the pampas with the vocal energy of an approaching football crowd. Individuals closer to my vantage point on the veranda made themselves known; they sounded like chainsaws with a small fleet of two-stroke mopeds as a backing. The variety of gratings and scrapings, rasping and sawing was extraordinary. I was astonished at the volume of noise an insect can generate. One band off to my left sounded like a gang of men with hacksaws working hard and fast to cut their way through prison bars. And all this cacophony was just to attract a mate, or maybe to defend a bit of territory.

But the concert had only begun. Now the frogs entered, adding a heavy wind section and some unruly percussion, each frog syncopating to a different rhythm, belching and burping their croaks with egocentric passion. Some frogs resonated like the lowest note on a double bass while others provided a touch of opera with child-like wails of deep and tragic disappointment.

I was delighted with this barrage of sound as nature gave vent to its own voice; and I reflected that these billions of 'singing' insects and frogs were the staple diet of all the magnificent birds I had come to see; the vermillion flycatcher, the tiger heron that stalked about the ranch, and the turkey-sized screamer who circled high in the sky at sunset with his mate, screaming a toneless duet.

Such concerts will have been performed nightly for many millions of years before human beings emerged and added their noise to the silence.

TACKLING NOISE IN DAILY LIFE

◆

The modern world (for those of us fortunate enough to live in affluence), with all its inventions and advantages, comforts and improved lifestyles, has become, we are occasionally forced to admit, unnecessarily noisy. This is sometimes the case when people give no thought to the peace and comfort of their neighbours.

CAR ALARMS AND SECURITY ALARMS; Christmas jingles in shops; loud music in pubs and the background chatter of TV; other people's heavy beat music late at night; small motorbikes punching way beyond their weight; low flying aircraft and traffic, traffic, traffic... We each have our own pet hate and example of unnecessary noise pollution. What can be done about it?

The first thing to be done, of course, is to see if the offending noise can be curbed. We should all lobby against noise pollution at every reasonable opportunity – but not in the spirit of grumpy old men or women at odds with the world, angry at its invasions. The modern world blesses many of us with a lifestyle that to our ancestors would be like paradise. Unnecessary noise, however, is just that – unnecessary.

Silence, Please!

It is easy to build up a head of steam about noisy neighbours, but more often than not they turn out to be perfectly reasonable and biddable if approached quietly and respectfully. And that motorbike that revs up at nightfall and roars all about the village lanes, disturbing the evening's tranquillity – well, the community police officer is the perfectly proper person to mention it to. A quiet word in the right place can solve many problems. We just need the courage and determination.

Many stores play music around Christmas, jingles that could drive you mad if you heard too much of it (how do the poor sales assistants survive six hours of 'Silent Night'?). Why not suggest to the manager a 'music-free' shopping evening?

And as for pubs – it is worth complimenting the manager or bartender if there is no piped music or distracting TV screen. They need feedback and will be warmed by support for their policy. The trouble with background music is that it becomes accepted in society as the default position. We owe it to ourselves and others to say if we prefer quietness.

Drastic Steps

Noise pollution in the poorer parts of our cities is a particular curse, and indeed a major social problem — neighbours are close and sometimes uncaring; walls are thin and there is no community code on how to behave. Other people's loud music at 4am in the morning can drive hard-working weary neighbours literally mad. Society needs to make some bold decisions here — police powers must be strengthened, and the police themselves should be educated to grasp the serious nature of the problem. The immediate confiscation of loud music equipment is a solution that has been successfully tried in some cities. Someone whose expensive equipment has been impounded will think twice before callously ignoring the natural rights of neighbours.

Noise pollution in the poorer parts of our cities is a particular curse.

A Mindful Way of Hearing

There are distracting noises, however, about which nothing can be done, apart from changing our attitude. This may involve the difficult task of 'standing back' and letting go of the anger and frustration the noise may generate within us.

I was in conversation once with a softly spoken Thai Buddhist. He was the archetypal monk, with simple flowing robe and gentle open smile – the very spirit of calmness. He was working temporarily in the Thai National Tourist office in London. I asked him how it was. 'Fine!' he answered, 'but my colleagues are having a bit of a problem just now.' 'How's that?' I queried. 'There's a building site next door and all day long they are demolishing what was there before. It is *very* noisy from all the heavy drilling. But I have meditated about it and decided I will think of the noise as an echo of the rock drills of the gods creating the world. Now I am happy with it!'

A New Attitude

It is a simple trick. No, 'trick' is not the word – it is more a mindful way of hearing. It involves adopting a new attitude, while understanding that true silence is an inner thing, something that, when you have discovered it, you can carry with you out into a noisy world.

I have tried my friend's mindful method myself. In the past I always found it hard to sleep on long-haul flights, confined to the limited space of an economy seat with the incessant roar of the aircraft engines. I would arrive at my destination groggy and discombobulated. Then I tried focusing on the sound rather than hating it – now, I shut my eyes and think myself into the forest by the great Iguazu waterfalls in Argentina. Millions of tonnes of white water cascade per minute over the rock ledges into the gorge below. The roar of the engines becomes the roar of the waterfalls. And I slip easily into sleep.

Inner Silence on the Street

Silence for me is being in a place where I do not have to talk to anyone and no one will talk to me. But there is another sort of silence that needs our mindful attention – the stilling of an agitated mind. This inner silence is even more important than physical quietness. I have always found that the very best way to settle the churning distractions of the mind is to open my mental windows and focus my attention on something external. We have a wood-burning stove now, and to stare into the flames and caverns of heat between the logs is a wonderful way to let go the chains of thought forged during the day. A candle flame, as I have found, can serve the same purpose. Paradoxically, I also find that, while I live in the country, a day up in London – dropping into an art gallery, strolling down a shopping street just looking at the people – is marvellously restful and brings its own inner silence.

FINDING THE INNER SILENCE

◆

Before we can carry our own inner silence out into the noisy world, we need to identify it, to know it as a friend. Everyone who has found this inner silence will have discovered it in their own different way. We can find it even when simply standing by a gatepost.

THERE WAS A MOTHER WITH THREE CHILDREN in my Yorkshire parish who worked in a local mill and inevitably lived a busy life. But she was calm and secure in herself. She explained, 'My husband goes off to work early, and then I have to give the children their breakfast before getting them off to school. When they are gone I have the house to myself for half an hour before I have to set off to work. That's *my* time. I drink a cup of tea and let the silence settle around me.'

Without practising a formal meditation, she had naturally discovered her own inner silence, and looked forward to it as a treat, reflected on it during the day, and cherished it.

We all owe it to ourselves to find these pauses in life and to cherish them. They may in fact be more common than we realize, but often we let them pass without acknowledgement.

'My Time'

I have been asking lots of friends recently about these silent moments and have been surprised at how many refer to them as '*My time*'. Anna, an elite athlete in Australia, used that term to describe her early-morning runs when preparing for a marathon. She calls it a 'non-methodical meditation', speaking in almost the language of mystics: 'I start with an empty mind, a void, and then I see a white horizontal line; I run under and through it and find a wonderful solitude.' Her daughter, Steph, swims several kilometres a day before heading off to work or college; without prompting, she said, 'I just love it – it's *my* time.'

My son Josh, who runs his own business, finds silence in the shower; with water pouring over his head, his mind can let go and be open to ideas. My daughter Imogen follows the Soka Gakkai path of Buddhism and finds (ironically, she observes) silence through chanting. She refers to it as mindful listening. 'There are seven Buddhists in my road in south London, so it is easy to find someone to chant with. There comes a point in the chanting when I begin to hear the overtones, which are very beautiful, and a huge space opens up in my mind, which is very still.'

Another person I talked to, who has lobbied often against the curse of noise pollution in cities, goes once a year to Verbier in the Alps, in July when the lower snow has melted. He walks. The silence in the high Alps is wonderful, he observed.

Peace on a Kibbutz
Long ago, I worked on a fish farm in Israel for six months. Life on a kibbutz is very communal, like a tightly packed village,

with everyone eating together in the central canteen. I shared a cabin with two other volunteers and we rose at five in the morning to work in the fishponds by the River Jordan in northern Galilee. I began to feel the need for some space and found that one can find silence anywhere.

I liked to spend twenty minutes or so a day meditating or saying prayers, which was hardly possible in the tight and rather public space of our cabin. So in the early evening I would wander down to a gate that led on into an orchard; no one was working on that part of the farm at that time of day. I could stand gazing across the valley to the hills of Judea for half an hour and see no one. And if someone did pass, then no matter, I was quietly admiring the view. I had found my private space, a moment of stillness and silence, just by standing by a gatepost. I came to value and cherish it greatly.

FINDING A PERSONAL NARRATIVE

One of the most important elements in getting to know oneself is being able to tell a confident story about who one is, and how one got to be here. This narrative begins with childhood, and at its best should have come to terms with any difficult times or traumas.

MANY PEOPLE HAVE DISCOVERED that an extended period of silent time, spent alone, has the tendency to awaken childhood memories that have either been forgotten or never been properly attended to. Sorting out the past, being pleased with it, or laying the bad bits to rest, is one of the best contributions we can make to our enjoyment of the present; it brings a sense of security, peace and confidence. To a great extent, we are defined by the memories and stories that make up our personal narratives. Linking them together is our enduring sense of self, that quiet inner reality that makes the seventy-year-old reflect that 'I don't feel any different now than I did when I was seventeen – or seven; just older and slower on the outside, with a few more aches and pains!'

A Journey Through the Past

The discovery of a coherent personal narrative extending right back to childhood is something Sara Maitland writes about in *A Book of Silence*. She reflects on the matter on a ten-day walk across the windblown solitary wastes of northern Galloway, the mountains and hills where she grew up. The activity of walking, she records, improved her memory. 'I had a very sharp recall of episodes, events and emotions... Things from far back in childhood.'

This was exactly my own experience when in student days I spent that somewhat misguided week up on Birker Moor, 'doing some writing'. I wrote about this seeming failure in chapter one, as an object lesson on how *not* to set about spending an extended period of time in solitary silence. But all the time I was there, sitting on rocks or wandering over the moors, my mind was going back over the past. At the time, I did not understand the significance of what was happening as I sorted out childhood memories.

Muddled Memories

My father was a restless man and we moved home many times in childhood. By the time I was five years old I had lived in six places around England. This is one reason my mental system needed some silence and solitude up on the moor. It wanted to get things straight – to sort out and put in order that jumble of internal 'snapshots'. My earliest memories dated back to my second year – the sound of air raid sirens in Bristol; walking with some adult in the Forest of Dean and seeing the white bones of a dead animal; dropping a woolly ball in a steep street of Cinderford in Gloucestershire and watching it roll away down the hill. They weren't unhappy memories at all, just muddled; and I was glad to identify them and place them in order – to find the roots to my story.

The whole process of thinking back through my life from childhood through adolescence to student days was healing and strengthening, giving me a much more confident sense of self, though I did not acknowledge it at the time.

Put in order that jumble of internal 'snapshots'.

TAKING TIME OUT TO MEDITATE

◆

We may find that it is not enough simply to locate pauses in the daily routine in our search for a more meaningful silence. We will then want to take a further step by being proactive and making time for silence on a regular basis.

A N OBVIOUS ROUTE TO SILENCE is through meditation. Many people practise this regularly and the results are always beneficial. Don't be daunted by the seriousness of the word or by not having a teacher – it is very easy. You can do it now. Later, if you hear of a good teacher locally, perhaps through a friend who meditates with a group, ask about it and if you like what you hear then join them.

Most good bookshops will have a shelf devoted to yoga, healthy living and meditation. Peruse the books and you will easily find one that will be a good guide for you. The best that I have found, anywhere, is *Meditation: An In-Depth Guide* by Ian Gawler and Paul Bedson. The authors teach a system they call MBSM: Mindfulness-Based Stillness Meditation. It is clearly written and tells you all you need to know.

Are You Sitting Comfortably?

Here are a few pointers to get you started:

• Aim to spend 10–15 minutes a day meditating, every day. That, in itself, will be an achievement.

- Try to stick to the same time – best in the morning and not after a heavy meal.
- Find a quiet place where you will not be interrupted.
- Be sure to wear comfortable clothing.
- Select a firm chair in which you can sit comfortably (*not* an armchair or sofa!) with feet flat on the floor and back held upright, hands in your lap with palms facing upwards if that comes easily.
- Close your eyes – or leave them open; whichever suits. Just rest your sight.
- Think your way around your body observing your posture, noticing where your feet are, how you are settled on the chair.
- Become aware of your breathing and follow the rise and fall of your lungs.
- Your thoughts will wander – this happens to everybody. Take notice of the thoughts and maybe tell them, 'Later!', then dismiss them. The aim eventually is to discover a quiet mind settled in its own silence.
- Don't expect anything startling – it is just you sitting quietly.
- Before you finish, give a thought to the day ahead, knowing that you can take this peace with you.

You will learn to remember the silence you find through this simple discipline when you return to the demands of the family or the busy challenges at work.

SILENCE & META-NARRATIVES

◆

It is a help in our quest for silence if we have a world view that gives some significance and meaning to our lives; if there is a story (which we probably share with others) that tells us why we are here and whether we have a purpose.

THERE IS A QUESTION THAT TROUBLES some religious people. Is it possible for people who seek silence through meditation to enjoy the inner solitude without having a religious faith or spiritual meta-narrative? By this I mean a religious world story that provides some idea of why we are here and where we are going; it is that greater narrative in which our own personal narratives play an integrated and meaningful part. In the Judeo-Christian tradition we have the story, through scripture, of God's revelation of Himself and his purposes for the world, focusing on the Torah for Jews and the figure of Jesus Christ for Christians; a story in which we have a part to play.

Spirituality Without Religion

The Buddhist has a reason for seeking silence through meditation – a mindful grasp of reality leads towards enlightenment and the blissful state of nirvana, that great awakening that is beyond words. The modern Christian, even if agnostic about Heaven as a state of being beyond death, nevertheless has a core belief in God, and the possibility of being held in God's love for eternity.

A contemporary meta-narrative can be spiritual, of course, without the definition of any particular religious tradition; it can make an inner assent to the view that life has spiritual meaning, and that this meaning has consequences for the way we live, recognizing the value of other people's lives and acknowledging that they too have their own inner worlds.

A Magnificent Story

Science, today, provides an alternative story that gives some meaning to our lives for those who do not belong to any religious tradition. The history of our cosmos is mind-blowing. Beginning in silence with a random quantum fluctuation in the void, the universe emerged from virtually 'nothing' to become the great expanding evolving 'something' that we observe today. In the rich biodiversity of the planet we inhabit, the cosmos explores through evolution all the rich potential of its remarkable self-assembling chemistry. This story is too magnificent to tell briefly. But here we are, you and I — and we are part of it; pioneers of evolving life, with awakening minds alert to the process that gave birth to us.

It would be hard *not* to be excited (whether with a religious faith or not) by meditating, in silence, on the remarkable circumstance of our own individual existence in the here-and-now. Just being alive and aware of it is a miracle.

INDEX

DEDICATION

❖

For my grandchildren – Rose, Sam and Layla.

SELECT BIBLIOGRAPHY

❖

The Collected Poems of George Mackay Brown by George Mackay Brown
(John Murray, 2005)

The Masks of God: Primitive Mythology by Joseph Campbell
(Souvenir Press Ltd, 1973)

Silence by Shusaku Endo (Penguin, 1988)

A Time to Keep Silence by Patrick Leigh Fermor
(New York Review Books, 2007)

Hermits: The Insights of Solitude by Peter France (Chatto and Windus, 1996)

Meditation: An In-Depth Guide by Ian Gawler and Paul Bedson
(Allen & Unwin, 2010)

Kilvert's Diary by Francis Kilvert (Jonathan Cape, 1960)

A Book of Silence by Sara Maitland (Granta, 2008)

Elected Silence by Thomas Merton (Hollis and Carter, 1949)

Zen and the Birds of Appetite by Thomas Merton (New Directions, 1968)

Sea Room: An Island Life in the Hebrides by Adam Nicolson
(North Point Press, 2002)

The Principal Upanishads by S. Radhakrishnan (Allen & Unwin Ltd, 1969)

Exploring the Book of Kells by George Otto Simms (The O'Brien Press, 1988)

Thoreau on Birds by Henry David Thoreau (Beacon Press, 1998)

Walden: or, Life in the Woods by Henry David Thoreau
(Sterling Innovation, 2009)

Tao Te Ching by Lao Tzu (Penguin Classics, 2000)